The authors

John Silvester has been a crime
reporter in Melbourne since 1978.
He worked for The Sunday Times
'Insight' team in London in 1990,
and has co-authored several crime
books, including the best-seller
Underbelly. He is currently Law and
Crime Editor for *The Age*.

Andrew Rule has been a journalist
since 1975 and has worked in
newspapers, television and radio.
He wrote *Cuckoo*, the true story of
the notorious 'Mr Stinky' case, and
has edited and published several
other books, including the original
Underbelly. He is a feature writer
for *The Age*.

They won the prestigious Ned Kelly
Award for True Crime writing for
Underbelly 3.

UNDERBELLY 4

TRUE CRIME STORIES

III.

UNDERBELLY 4

Published in Australia by
Floradale Productions Pty Ltd and Sly Ink Pty Ltd
November 2000
Reprinted March 2002, January 2006, August 2008

Distributed wholesale by
Gary Allen Pty Ltd,
9 Cooper Street,
Smithfield, NSW
Telephone 02-9725 2933

Underbelly 4
True Crime Stories

ISBN – 0958 6071 6 8

Cover design by committee. Cover artwork by Dean
Muller of Dean's Screens, Golden Square
Typesetting and layout by Write Impression Publishing

CONTENTS

CHAPTER 1

Pure Evil

*'It's too late, Pam, I can't stop now.
They will lock me up.'*

THE old bluestone court house in Bendigo is one of the most imposing in Victoria. On the first floor is the main court room, with a large oil painting of an English lord hanging on the rear wall and a huge chandelier over the bar table.

But on this day the case did not fit the majesty of the surroundings. Standing in the dock was a plump, nondescript man facing the relatively minor charge of false imprisonment.

The accused wasn't even going to fight, having earlier agreed to plead guilty to the solitary charge. This would save court time and public money, allow the female victim to avoid the trauma of giving evidence and enable the justice system to move on to the next, and seemingly more important, case.

But the accused was not motivated by remorse. He had a powerful incentive to plead guilty to this one charge. In return the prosecution had agreed to drop more serious charges, including kidnap, assault with a weapon and indecent assault.

The man in the dock was Peter Norris Dupas. And, for all his mild looks, he had a history of committing increasingly violent sexual crimes over four decades. At least one policeman and an experienced psychiatrist warned years earlier he was a potential killer, but that didn't stop Dupas being allowed to plead to the least significant charge of those laid against him.

The year before his trial, the Victorian Government had passed a controversial law that enabled courts to sentence criminals such as Dupas to indefinite jail terms. The law was to protect the community from serial sex offenders – and if there was a stereotype of the man the Act was designed to catch, it was Dupas. But for the law to be activated the offender had to found guilty of a so-called 'serious offence'. Unlawful imprisonment fell just short – it was considered too minor for the draconian legislation.

It would have not seemed a minor offence to the twenty-six year old woman Dupas had attacked and slashed in the public toilets at Lake Eppalock in January, 1994. Dupas was wearing a balaclava when he followed the woman into the toilet block, where he threatened her and cut her with a knife. He clearly intended to rape her before he was frightened off. In the boot of his car were handcuffs, knives … and, chillingly, a shovel. A weapon might conceivably be used only to frighten someone – but a shovel has only one use for a violent abductor. To bury a body.

Defence and prosecution lawyers do deals all the time. In this case Dupas's lawyer made it clear his client would plead to 'appropriate' charges. Perhaps the evidence would not support the more serious charges, and jury trials are always a risk, but there can be no doubt the defence lawyer did well to cut a deal for his client. He was aware that a guilty plea to unlawful imprisonment would save Dupas from the risk of going to jail forever.

In the Bendigo Court on 18 August, 1994, Judge Leo Hart was also interested in whether he could deal with Dupas under the indefinite sentence rules. He asked: 'Is the offence for which he has pleaded guilty, an offence which, together with his prior convictions, brings into play ...'

Defence lawyer: 'No.'

Judge Hart: 'The provisions introduced by the Sentencing (Amendment) Act 1993?'

Defence lawyer: 'No, it is not, Your Honour.'

With his record Dupas was going to go to jail, anyway. The trouble was, it wouldn't be for long enough. He was sentenced to three years and nine months with a minimum of two.

He was released from jail on 29 September, 1996, and would go on to kill one and possibly three women. He was convicted in August 2000 of the murder of psychotherapist Nicole Patterson, who was stabbed to death in her Westgarth home on 19 April, 1999.

He is is also strongly suspected of killing Margaret Maher, who was killed in October, 1997, and Mersina Halvagis, who was stabbed to death in the Fawkner Cemetery while tending her grandmother's grave in November, 1997.

PETER Norris Dupas was just fifteen and still in school uniform when he first attacked a woman with a knife. Now, more than thirty years later, police believe he might be one of Australia's worst serial killers.

Dupas is a criminal oddity that the criminal justice system could not handle. A man considered sufficiently mentally twisted to need treatment, yet too 'sane' to be institutionalised for life.

The police, prison officers and many of the psychiatrists who knew Dupas wrote reports suggesting he would re-offend, yet he was released from jail to do just that.

An insignificant little man, who was once a fat, lonely school-boy, he has carried a knife since he was a teenager, and attacked women whenever he has had the opportunity.

3

And, like many serial offenders, his crimes have become progressively more violent, despite medical and psychiatric treatment since the 1960s.

Dupas was born in Sydney and his family moved to Melbourne when he was a baby. His brother and sister were years older than him and he was effectively treated as an only child by his mother and father, who were old enough to be his grandparents.

He was later to say he was spoiled when he was growing up. He went to Waverley High School, repeated year seven and was seen as a slow learner with no friends and an unhealthy array of complexes.

'He did not participate in sports and describes himself as having been very obese and the subject of ridicule by his school mates,' concluded a psychiatrist who examined him in 1990.

It was in October, 1968, that Peter Dupas first showed his dark side.

A female neighbour had returned home a few weeks earlier after having a baby when she heard a knock on her back door. It was Dupas, wearing his Waverley High School uniform.

'Young Peter Dupas got on very well with my husband and he used to call in to our house and talk with us,' she would later tell police.

The boy asked if he could borrow a small knife to peel some vegetables. 'I remarked to him about him peeling the potatoes for his mother and what a good boy he was.'

Then Dupas suddenly attacked her, slashing her fingers, neck and face. As he tried to stab her he said: 'It's too late, Pam, I can't stop now. They will lock me up.'

Finally, he stopped and began to cry. When asked by police why he had attacked the woman he said, 'I must have been trying to kill her or something. I didn't know why I was trying to do this, as far as I am concerned there is no reason for me to do anything to Pam but I could not help myself.' He was put on probation for eighteen months and given psychiatric treatment.

Like many loners who turn into sex offenders, the nerdish and spoiled Dupas craved power, and like many serial killers he applied and was rejected from the police force. He was one centimetre too short.

According to a former FBI crime profiler, John Douglas, 'frequently serial offenders had failed in their efforts to join police departments ... one of their main fantasy occupations is police officers.'

In the next few years Dupas began a pattern of low level sex-related crimes. He was found hiding in the back yard of an Oakleigh house as he watched a woman undress in March, 1972. Two years later he was caught in the female toilet block at the McCrae Caravan Park watching women shower.

He was seen to follow women and young girls and his behaviour became increasingly aggressive.

In 1973 he began to attack women in their own homes. He would knock on the door, pretend to have car trouble and then ask to borrow a screwdriver. In one case he threatened to hurt a woman's baby if she attempted to struggle against him.

It was during this investigation that police started to believe Dupas was in a league of his own. It was not the crime he committed – violent as it was – nor his looks, as he appeared quite harmless.

It was the way he answered or, more accurately, didn't answer questions, that worried detectives.

Senior Detective Ian Armstrong interviewed him at the Nunawading police station on 30 November, 1973. Dupas was twenty-one and looked younger. He had a pudgy, baby face and the manner of a person who lacked resolve.

To Armstrong he looked the sort of suspect who would easily crack under questioning. But as everyone who was to deal with

Dupas over the next twenty-seven years would find, looks can deceive.

Many experienced criminals know how to lie their way through a police interview but a frightened young man usually confesses quickly. Dupas was different – dangerously so.

'We tried everything and he would get to the point where he was about to talk. Then something would snap and he would go blank, then deny everything,' recalled Armstrong, a senior sergeant at Warrnambool when Dupas was found guilty of murder.

'He stood out. To me the guy was just pure evil. He committed a rape in Mitcham and would have committed more given the opportunity. He looked so innocuous but he was a cold, calculating liar.

'His attacks were all carefully planned and he showed no remorse. We could see where he was going. I remember thinking, "this guy could go all the way" (to murder).'

Dupas was being interviewed over the Mitcham rape, which had happened six days earlier. 'It wasn't me, I didn't do it ... I don't know anything about the incident ... She must have been mixed up with someone else,' were his answers. Nobody believed him.

He was convicted in 1974 over rape and burglary charges and sentenced to nine years with a minimum of five.

Ian Armstrong felt worried enough about the young offender to write a report which said in part: 'He is an unmitigated liar... he is a very dangerous young person who will continue to offend where females are concerned and will possibly cause the death of one of his victims if he is not straightened out.'

In his first few months in custody Dupas was examined by one of Australia's most experienced psychiatrists, Dr Allen Bartholomew. He noted that Dupas refused to admit his problems. 'I am reasonably certain that this youth has a serious psycho-sexual problem, that he is using the technique of denial as a coping device and that he is to be seen as potentially dangerous. The denial technique makes for huge difficulty in treatment.'

Late in 1977, a group of parents who lived near the Dupas family in Mount Waverley contacted the Parole Board and urged that he not be released, as they believed he was still dangerous.

But Dupas started to learn how to play the system. According to Bartholomew, he began to talk about his crimes, not because he wanted to be treated but because he wanted to get out of jail to re-offend. 'I feel that when he realised that his hopes for parole might be jeopardised by his denials, he began to admit his guilt.'

Despite a warning by Bartholomew in September, 1978, that Dupas 'was a danger to female society' he was released from prison on 4 September, 1979. Within two months he attacked four women in just ten days.

On 9 November, 1979, he forced his way into a toilet block in Frankston and raped a woman. Two days later he chased a woman and threatened her with a knife. On 18 November he dragged an elderly woman into a vacant block and stabbed her, and the following day he attacked another woman in the same area. In each attack he wore a balaclava and carried a knife.

He told police, 'I've had this problem for about six years. I'm glad I got caught.'

Bartholomew could not resist pointing out that his view had been ignored. 'The present offences are exactly what might have been predicted,' he wrote when Dupas was again charged with rape and assault.

He concluded that Dupas was unlikely to change. The trained psychiatrist and the experienced detective, Ian Armstrong, both saw something in this harmless looking man that compelled them to commit to paper their fears that he was a potential killer. Bartholomew warned that Dupas's increasingly violent rapes and knife attacks 'could have fatal consequences.'

Even parole officers who had believed Dupas could change began to give up hope.

'There is little that can be said in Dupas' favour. He remains an extremely disturbed, immature and dangerous man. His release on parole was a mistake,' according to a report added to his file in September, 1980.

Dupas was found guilty of rape, malicious wounding, assault with intent to rob and indecent assault for the 1979 attacks. He was sentenced to six and a half years jail with a five-year minimum.

It was to become a pattern. Dupas would do what he was told in jail, attend the courses, do the therapy and appear to be changing, only to attack women whenever he was out of jail.

He was released again on 27 February, 1985, although no-one seriously believed he would not attack again. It didn't take long. On 3 March he raped a twenty one-year-old woman who was sunbathing at Rye ocean beach.

After the beach attack he gave police his trademark speech of remorse: 'I'm sorry for what happened. Everyone was telling me I'm okay now. I never thought it was going to happen again. All I wanted to do is live a normal life.'

He was sentenced to twelve years with a minimum of ten. The beach rape was near the spot where a woman sunbather had been bashed and murdered in remarkably similar circumstances only weeks earlier.

Helen McMahon was bashed to death on the Rye back beach on 13 February that year. Her body had been found naked, covered only by a towel, and her murder was never solved.

A counsellor who tried to help Dupas wrote, 'Through long-term association with various professionals he has learned to manipulate any individual who has endeavoured to challenge his offending behaviour by way of saying the right things and behaving in a convincing manner in a supervised environment.'

Despite the treatment his crimes became more violent. Despite his repeated claims he was dealing with his problems, he just became more cunning.

While in jail Dupas met and married a female nurse, sixteen years his senior. They married in Castlemaine Jail in 1987 while he was still a prisoner.

He told parole officers his marriage to a 'beautiful person' would help him stop sexually offending. It didn't.

He was released in March, 1992, and in January, 1994, he attacked a woman at knife point in a toilet block at Lake Eppalock.

The woman's boyfriend, an off-duty Australian Federal Police officer, grabbed Dupas after a car chase. He was held until two Victoria Police arrived. He even whined pathetically, 'They're hurting me!' while he was pinned as the police approached. He was found guilty only of false imprisonment and given a two-year minimum.

Dupas was released again in September, 1996, and eventually moved into a house in Coanne Street, Pascoe Vale – near a shopping strip in Cumberland Road.

Margaret Maher, a local prostitute, regularly went shopping in Cumberland Road. That is, until she was abducted and murdered in October, 1997.

About a month later Mersina Halvagis was stabbed to death in the Fawkner Cemetery while she was visiting her grandmother's grave. Dupas's grandfather is buried at Fawkner in the same area.

EVERYBODY liked Nicole Patterson. She was a psycho-therapist who devoted much of her time trying to help with young people with drug problems. Those who knew her described a vibrant and compassionate young woman. Her sister, Kylie, said, 'She was the most beautiful person I've known and she had a lot of special gifts that not many people have.'

In early 1999, Ms Patterson, then twenty eight, decided to broaden her client base and converted the front bedroom of her house in Harper Street, Westgarth, into a consulting room.

She began to advertise in local newspapers. On 3 March a man calling himself 'Malcolm' telephoned. Over the next five weeks he was to ring her fifteen times before he made an appointment for 19 April.

Malcolm said he wanted to be treated for depression. He didn't say he was a violent sex offender. Ms Patterson wrote the name 'Malcolm' and his mobile telephone number in her diary and circled the time of 9am on 19 April.

Police believe Dupas knocked on the door at 9am and was ushered into the consulting room. Ms Patterson made plunger coffee and entered the room with cups, sugar and milk. Then, without warning, he attacked, stabbing her repeatedly.

She managed to scratch his face and yell before she was overwhelmed.

What followed was almost beyond belief in its savagery. But, despite his frenzy, Dupas's cold-blooded instinct for self-preservation asserted itself. After the murder he searched the house for any evidence that he had been there. He missed her diary, which was under clothing on the couch in the living room.

It would lead police to him.

When police raided his home three days later they found the newspaper advertisement for Ms Patterson's psychotherapy sessions with her name handwritten by Dupas on the border.

They also found a blood-splattered jacket. DNA tests established the blood was 6.53 billion times more likely to have come from Ms Patterson 'than from an individual female chosen at random from the Victorian Caucasian population.' They also found a black balaclava and a front page of the *Herald Sun* report on the murder. The picture of Nicole Patterson had been slashed with a knife.

The head of the investigation, Detective Senior Sergeant Jeff Maher, is used to dealing with killers, but he found Dupas unsettling. 'He was pure evil. He was not physically intimidating but he really sent shivers up your spine.'

Maher said Dupas refused to talk of the crime or co-operate with the investigation in any way. 'Nothing he did was on impulse. Everything was planned in the most calculating manner.'

FBI expert John Douglas says each serial killer has a 'signature' that links his murder victims. Nicole Patterson and Margaret Maher were killed in almost identical ways.

There is also evidence to suggest a connection with the way Mersina Halvagis was killed in the Fawkner Cemetery in 1997.

Nicole Patterson wore a silver choker-style necklace. When police found it next to her body it had been broken and repaired with sticky tape. Friends who saw Nicole the night before the murder said the necklace was then intact. Detectives believe the killer may have ripped it from her and worn it himself while he was in the house.

Police said many of his attacks were concentrated on the breast area of his victims.

The doctor who examined Dupas when he was arrested said he was 'an anxious, timid-looking man wearing bifocals. I noted that he had prominent deposits over the pectors muscles which had the appearance of female breasts.'

BILL Patterson and George Halvagis were old mates. They watched their children grow up together when they lived in

Warracknabeal, in country Victoria, in the 1970s.

But, like many families that move to big cities, they lost touch over the years. Now they are linked by a shared grief.

Both men have had to deal with the death of a daughter. In both cases they were murdered and now, in a bizarre coincidence, it appears both women were killed by the same man.

In August, 2000, Bill Patterson and George Halvagis sat in the public gallery of Court Four in the Supreme Court and watched as Dupas, forty seven, was convicted of killing Nicole Patterson.

George and his wife Christina sat in the back of the court and watched most of the seven-day trial. Police were concerned the grieving couple were there to take justice into their own hands. On the last day of the trial police checked them for weapons before they were allowed into the court.

'I do not know why they would do that. We were here to support Bill and his family, not to do anything to the man who was charged,' Mr Halvagis said later.

'We were old friends and now it may be that the same animal killed our daughters.'

If the accused man knew who was behind him he didn't show any concern. He sat in the dock looking straight ahead. Dressed in a blue suit and a 1970s style tie, he looked composed, his hands resting on his lap.

Only the occasional fidget with his thumbs betrayed any sign of nerves. He looked harmless enough, the sort who might be given the role of the librarian in an amateur play. But his looks belied his criminal history.

When the jury began to file in to hear the judge's final summary Dupas was on his feet, even before the court was asked to rise. Dupas didn't need to be told – he knew the rules because he had been in the criminal dock many times before.

The Patterson family sat through the whole trial. They listened to evidence about how Nicole died, about her last moments. They learned facts that grieving relatives should never have to hear.

George Halvagis is driven man, but not a vindictive one. He says he is not looking for revenge, only justice. He too, sat through the entire trial and, like the Pattersons, he wept after the jury found Dupas guilty. The Pattersons cried because they finally knew what happened to their daughter, the Halvagises because they still don't know for certain what happened to theirs.

George Halvagis has one dream left. He wants the man who killed his daughter to be put in the dock in the Supreme Court and stand trial. 'I don't want anyone to harm him (Dupas) in prison. I want him to live so we can find out what happened to Mersina.'

THE police also have unfinished business and unanswered questions. They want to talk to Dupas about the murders of Mersina Halvagis and Margaret Maher.

Homicide detectives got the court's permission to speak to Dupas over the Halvagis murder while he was in custody but he still refused to co-operate.

In any case, Dupas's arrest record would indicate he is unlikely to talk. The days of heavy-handed police interviews are long gone and an investigation based on the need to gain a confession is usually flawed. Police need evidence that cannot be later recanted.

The former head of the homicide squad, Carl Mengler, who retired as a Deputy Commissioner, believes juries should know when a suspect refuses to answer questions.

'In a murder case the formal interview is video taped. Why not play it to the jury? If the suspect declines to answer questions then let the jury see it. If the police are unfair in the interview then the jury would know from watching the tape. If juries are to make decisions based on the facts then let them have all the facts, in fairness to both the defence and the prosecution.

'A suspect does not have to answer questions but a jury should be aware of what they have and haven't said.'

WHAT makes a man evil? Peter Dupas was not beaten as a child. He did not come from a broken home. His only complaint was that he was spoiled by his elderly parents.

Some men are driven to greatness, others can never overcome their compulsions.

Another sex offender, Ian Melrose Patterson, cut a nipple off one of his victims and slashed her more than 250 times. In his cell he collected pictures of Princess Di and Jana Wendt and in each picture he would cut off the nipples. He drew elaborate pictures of naked women tied up while in jail and yet he was released after serving his bare minimum sentence.

When freed in 1992 he was found to have inoperable cancer. He had tumours in his liver, kidneys, lungs, bones and chest wall. When he was released from hospital he went straight out and bought eight bondage books and a boning knife. He told associates he intended to commit more sex crimes before he died. 'What has been done can be done again. I have thought about it. They will have to take me out with a bullet this time,' he said.

He sexually assaulted a woman with a knife two weeks after he was diagnosed as terminally ill.

When he returned to hospital he was so sick that he needed constant oxygen. Even then he wouldn't stop, removing his mask to sexually harass the nursing staff. Eventually only male nurses would treat him. Only when he lapsed into a coma was he no longer a risk to women.

It would be convenient to blame someone for Dupas's life and, by extension, Nicole Patterson's death. But no judge gave him an unrealistically light sentence and no jury ignored compelling evidence. Every time he was charged with a serious sexual offence he was convicted. The problem was, while many in authority believed he would one day kill, they appeared powerless to stop him.

Nicole Patterson's sister, Kylie Nicholas, said that while the family was relieved when Dupas was found guilty they still felt betrayed by a criminal justice system that freed Dupas when it was almost certain he would attack again.

'Why did they let him out? I just don't understand the system. I only hope that people listen so this never happens again.'

AFTER being found guilty of the murder of Nicole Patterson, Peter Norris Dupas was sentenced to life in jail.

Justice Frank Vincent told him, 'You must, as a consequence of the commission of this terrible crime which has brought you before this court, be removed permanently from the society upon whose female members you have preyed for over thirty years.

'The sentence of this court is that you be imprisoned for the rest of your natural life and without the opportunity for release on parole.'

Justice Vincent was a criminal barrister who specialised in murder cases, he is an experienced Supreme Court Judge and chairman of the Parole Board. He has probably seen more killers than anyone in Australia.

During his closing remarks he captured the mood of the wider public in one sentence.

'At a fundamental level, as human beings, you present for us the awful, threatening and unanswerable question: How did you come to be as you are?'

(1)

Particulars as known regarding the death of
Raymond Patrick BENNETT @ CHUCK who was shot
at the City Magistrate's Court on 12th Nov. 1979.

(This document typed at 3pm on 12/11/79)

BRIEF PARTICULARS : The deceased appeared before the Melbourne
Magistrate's Court at 10am on Monday, 12th November 1979 where
he was facing committal proceedings on two counts of armed
robbery.   His case was referred from the main court to the
10th Court which is on the first floor.   Whilst being escorted
to this court at about 10.20am he was confronted by an armed
man who fired three shots at him.   The deceased, after receiving
a gunshot wound to his chest and hand ran down a flight of stairs
into the courtyard where he collapsed into the arms of two
uniformed policemen.   He was assisted to a corridor which is
near the entrance to the main court where he received medical
treatment before being transferred by ambulance to St Vincents
Hospital where he died about an hour later.

ESCORTING MEMBERS :   Senior Detective Peter John MUGAVIN 17772
                      Senior Detective Philip Joseph GLARE 17101.
                      Both members are from the Consorting Squad.
                      MUGAVIN was holding deceased when he was
shot.   GLARE was in the immediate vicinity.   Both these members
made an effort to intercept the offender who threatened them with
a .38 revolver.

OFFENDER :   Escaped immediately after the shooting by
going down a back stairway which leads through the Magistrate's
Car Park, from where he entered the rear of the Police Garage
which houses some police vehicles.   A galvinised iron sheet had

(2)

**The first police report into Bennett's murder, completed
within five hours of the hit. More than twenty years later
the courtroom killing remains unsolved.**

CHAPTER 2

Well Executed

'I've been shot in the heart.'

THE man in the dock knows there's a bullet out there somewhere with his name on it. But he doesn't know it's already in the hitman's revolver, and there's an itchy finger on the trigger, counting down the minutes.

His name is Raymond Patrick Bennett, also known as Ray Chuck, and he has just stepped into the old Melbourne Magistrates Court from the holding cells.

If he's worried, it doesn't show on his boxer's face, almost handsome despite its broken nose sprinkled with freckles and the dark eyes set in a hard gaze. It's a face that doesn't quite match the bold check jacket with the leather elbow patches, which looks like something a jackaroo might buy in a reckless moment on a city holiday.

At thirty one, Bennett might be the most dashing Australian crook of his generation, but a reputation like that wins enemies, and he has plenty. So many that, for seven weeks before this day, he has pointedly avoided bail, preferring the predictable discomforts of the Pentridge remand yards to his chances on the outside. He's always been game, but not foolhardy.

Still, he ought to feel safe here, in court, surrounded by dozens of people – including lawyers and policemen – and just across the road from Russell Street police headquarters. But he doesn't.

He has told his lawyer, who waits above, that he wants his wife kept away from the public areas of the court. He has taken out a huge life insurance policy, asking if the company will pay if he's 'shot walking down the street'. Months earlier, he sent his young son overseas to keep him out of danger. In one of the court cells reached through the door behind him is a message freshly written on the wall: RAY CHUCK, YOU WILL GET YOUR'S IN DUE COURSE YOU FUCKEN DOG.

Everybody knows he is a target. Except, it seems, the police whose job it is to know.

Bennett is in court for committal on armed robbery charges over a $69,000 payroll heist in Yarraville. A magistrate has to weigh the evidence to judge if he should be tried in a higher court.

Like all prisoners in custody who have to front a magistrate, he has been brought in through the Court One dock. Committals are automatically adjourned to one of the two courts upstairs, in a double-storey extension behind the main court.

Depending on who's telling the story, three – or perhaps two – detectives escort Bennett past the crowded bench seats and people standing at the back of the room, and into the open courtyard for the short walk to the stairs leading to courts ten and eleven.

By coincidence, there is a union demonstration at Trades Hall a block away and 167 officers have been called out, leaving Russell Street short of the uniformed police who usually escort prisoners. Which is why, it is later explained, two consorting squad detectives called Glare and Strang are asked to help an armed robbery detective, John Mugavin, to escort Bennett.

As Bennett and his escort walk past, a young constable waiting to give evidence mistakes the well-dressed robber for another detective. It's easy to see why. The dashing crook is a cut above the crowd in the court yard.

The nineteenth century court is Dickensian, and Hogarth could draw those waiting their turn in the dock. There are pimps, prostitutes, thieves, vagrants, drunks, louts and lost souls from the seedy side of a big city – the bad, the sad and the slightly mad, all chain smoking in the court yard. Bit players in this depressing daily drama, they watch surreptitiously as Bennett the underworld star is led past, through the doors and upstairs to his fate …

A minute later, three shots crash through the buzz of muttered conversations. There is a clatter of footsteps in the sudden silence. Someone upstairs yells: 'It's a .38. Get a gun!' Then the screaming starts.

A young *Age* reporter in the main court looks at his watch and scrawls down the time. It is 10.17am on that Monday morning, six days after the 1979 Melbourne Cup.

WHEN he heard the shots Constable Chris Carnie jumped up from his bench in the courtyard. So did Constable Alan Hill, who'd been waiting nervously to give evidence in the first case of his new career.

The two uniformed officers ran to the door leading to the stairs. Later, they gave slightly different accounts of where Bennett was standing, but it was probably on the landing between the first and second flight of steps. What neither ever forgets is that he had his arms crossed over his chest, and was bleeding from wounds in both hands. He said: 'I've been shot in the heart.'

19

Carnie caught Bennett as his legs buckled. He and Hill carried him through the courtyard and into the tiled vestibule outside the clerk's office near the Russell Street doorway. Hill, a former Navy medic, tried mouth to mouth and heart massage. He knew it was no use. A bullet had burst the pulmonary artery; Bennett was drowning in his own blood.

Bennett's lawyer, Joe Gullaci, rushed downstairs with the dying man's wife, Gail. He pushed the stricken woman (he describes her years later as 'incredibly brave') into the clerk's office so she couldn't see the wounds. An ambulance came, but police stopped the pair getting in it to go to St Vincent's hospital. They jumped in a police car, but the driver took them in exactly the wrong direction – towards Elizabeth Street.

It was symbolic, perhaps, of the way the whole affair was handled. Except by the gunman, whose timing and preparation seemed almost too good to be true.

A court reporter for *The Sun* newspaper, Julie Herd, had sat briefly on a bench beside the man before going into court ten to wait for the case to begin. She assumed he was a lawyer. He had gold-rimmed glasses, a full head of hair and a beard. He appeared calm and was dressed, she thought, in a dark blue suit.

One of the two consorting squad detectives with Bennett, Phil Glare, also took the man to be a solicitor. Glare said the man walked towards Bennett, looked at him and said, 'Cop this, you mother-fucker' as he drew a snub-nosed revolver from inside his coat and fired three shots.

Bennett turned and ran down the stairs. Glare yelled, 'He's off, Grab him!' Mugavin chased Bennett, assuming the shots were blanks and that it was an escape attempt, he later said.

Glare moved towards the gunman, who pointed the pistol at him and warned: 'Don't make me do it.' According to later coronial evidence, Glare's colleague Paul Strang was inside the courtroom, where he helped Detective Sergeant Noel Anderson remove a pistol – allegedly used in Bennett's armed robbery – from an exhibit bag.

Meanwhile, the gunman had threatened a civilian witness, Raymond Aarons, ('Move and I'll blow your fucking head off') then waited to see if anyone was going to follow him and slipped through a side door leading down a maze of back stairs and passages to a tin shed behind the police garage. An inspector, Bill Horman, held the door shut, fearing the gunman was trapped and would try to come out. When Anderson produced the exhibit pistol, Horman opened the door and Anderson rushed through.

But, by then, the gunman was long gone – through a hole already carefully prepared in the corrugated iron shed wall. The hole opened into a carpark at the neighbouring Royal Melbourne Institute of Technology. It was the perfect escape route – and it reeked of an inside job. Whoever did it had an expert knowledge of the court and the police carpark, or easy access to people who did have such knowledge.

By the time Bennett was pronounced dead an hour later, the rumor mill was humming. Frantic reporters with deadlines for the year's biggest crime story quoted unnamed police sources suggesting an 'outside' hitman was paid big money – the mooted sum was $50,000 – to do the killing.

But before the last edition of *The Herald* had hit the streets a different story was circulating inside Russell Street. At 2pm the head of the consorting squad, Angus Ritchie, took a call from an informer claiming the hit had been organised inside his own squad.

Some squad members jokingly encouraged the rumors in the police club that night. 'We couldn't buy a drink for a week,' recalls a retired detective who still doesn't fancy being named over the incident. 'Half the force thought we did it.'

Within days, the squad members would regret feeding the

rumors because one detective was told there was a contract on his life to avenge Bennett's death. He carried a gun for two years.

Detectives, unable to protect Bennett when he was alive, were given orders to guard his corpse. They were instructed to go to the North Melbourne funeral home where the body was lying after police heard his enemies planned to break-in, cut his hands off and send them to his wife.

Meanwhile, the public was still being fed the company line of a contract killer. Details of the more sinister theory, involving police, were not made public until the inquest finally began in March, 1981. But that was later.

TO his friends, Ray Bennett was tough, loyal, and good company. His lawyer, Joe Gullaci, liked him – though he admits Bennett and his mates were 'big kids with guns', professional armed robbers who terrified people and wouldn't hesitate to shoot rivals.

'These blokes were pretty good at their trade – in and out quickly (on robberies) and no shots fired and no drugs – unlike the current crop running around using their own product. It seemed to me they were thieves with some honor,' the hard-bitten Gullaci recalls. It was this 'honour' that eventually got Bennett killed. There were other reasons, too.

One was the 'Great Bookie Robbery' of 21 April, 1976. It later became well-known – and the subject of a television mini-series – that Bennett planned it, flying secretly to Australia for a few days while on pre-release leave from a prison on the Isle of Wight. He and his friend, Brian O'Callaghan, had led the 'Kangaroo Gang', robbing jewellery shops all over Europe.

Six of Bennett's team robbed bookmakers on settling day at the Victorian Club, then in Queen Street. A seventh man, in Pentridge at the time, received his share of a haul that was somewhat greater than the official figure of $1.4 million, because of undeclared cash bets.

The robbery earned Bennett and his crew the unwanted attention of people who wanted to redistribute their wealth, some of them willing to use boltcutters and blowtorches. There was even a plot by former friends to sell out the gang to the insurance underwriters saddled with the massive loss.

Police, bookmakers, and other criminals suddenly had several million reasons to resent Bennett. Tension rose between Bennett's crew and a group of painters and dockers led by the Kane brothers, Brian, Les and Ray. Certain members of the consorting squad backed the Kanes, standover men who had controlled 'ghosting' rackets on the wharves for years.

Those who took part deny this was the corrupt alliance it appears. As one longtime underworld observer notes: 'The squarehead world sees only the blue water on top, not the sharks underneath.' From the viewpoint of some consorting squad detectives, whose job was to swim with the sharks, it was necessary to keep one group of man-eaters where they could see them.

The 'consorters' were feared in the 1970s. Squad members called themselves the 'Fletcher Jones' boys – because, the joke went, like the clothing store of that name, they could 'fit anybody.' Before DNA testing, target profiling and flow charts, they gathered intelligence in pubs, nightclubs and race tracks.

Their brief was to know what heavy criminals were up to, and to act first to prevent crimes. Their tool-of-trade – apart from sledgehammers, planted 'throwaway' guns, unsigned statements and illegal telephone taps – was the draconian consorting law (now no longer regularly used) that meant that if a known criminal was caught consorting with another known criminal both could be charged and jailed.

Squad members worked unsupervised, in small groups. Many

socialised with criminals and had their own favourites. They were used as trouble shooters by some senior police who turned a blind eye to methods used. Some of them found the people they thought were the villains and then either massaged or fabricated evidence to suit their conclusions. Sometimes they were right.

One offender who'd been shot while being arrested – the kidnapper Edwin John Eastwood – had his wounded leg stretched in hospital to force him to talk.

It was an era when some of the heavy squads made their own rules and exacted severe punishment for any outsider who broke them. When one of the Kane brothers pulled up at the lights, and noticed an off-duty detective with his heavily pregnant wife in car next to him, he made a mistake that was to cost him several months in jail. Kane wound his window down and threatened the policeman, using a string of profanities. The detective quietly told him he was going too far, but the hyped-up Kane did not see the danger signs.

It was late December when the detective's squad mates caught up with Kane. They presented the career criminal with several sticks of gelignite, neatly wrapped in Christmas paper. As soon as he saw the gift he knew the evidence against him would be overwhelming. He didn't need a forensic report to know his fingerprints would be all over the package ... they had taken the paper from a drawer in Kane's flat and gift wrapped it in front of him.

After he was charged he told a senior policeman, 'I knew I shouldn't have shot my mouth off.' The policeman responded, 'You take one of this squad on, you take all of us on.'

It was around the same time that a known hitman had accepted a contract, but police didn't know who was the target or when the murder would take place. To stop the shooting a detective simply walked up to the hitman, gave him an unloaded gun and said, 'this is yours, Ron.' The contract killer was charged with being a felon in possession of a firearm. The hit was never carried out.

In the interview room a suspect who answered a question with the expression 'no comment' could soon find that it was more an opening statement in protracted negotiations than a concluding remark.

One detective, annoyed that his suspect refused to make a statement, removed his size fourteen boot, claiming it was his shoe phone. He put it to his ear – then turned to the suspect and said – 'It's for you' – before beating the man around the head with the boot. The suspect then began to answer questions. Every time the answers weren't correct the detective would again remove his boot, claiming he was taking another call. The suspect would then begin to answer questions again.

In another interview an armed robber refused to talk. Finally, a naked detective ran into the room and hit him around the head. The suspect, possibly more frightened of being confronted by a naked, overweight detective than the beating, confessed readily.

While most squads at the time bent the rules to suit themselves the consorting squad had made it an art-form. Consorters, whose job it was to go to places where criminals hung out, combined business and pleasure for fun and profit. Some race clubs were so grateful to have them on course that they slung them payments paid in plain envelopes ... written off as security payments which, of course, they were. The money was put in a slush fund largely used to entertain interstate detectives who would always arrive thirsty and hungry.

The consorters didn't like critics. When a former criminal and prison activist, Joey Hamilton, publicly complained about some of their methods, two squad members went to his house in Carlton and blew it up with explosives, a retired detective told the authors. When Hamilton said he believed the police were responsible for the attack, few believed him – but he was right.

'It was a different time,' the retired detective says nostalgically, before offering the opinion that the Walsh Street murders – and the consequent mayhem – would have been prevented if consorters had still been working.

This was the consorting squad before the police hierarchy decided that its dogs of war were out of control and disbanded it. Some consorters acted as judge and jury. The question is: were they also prepared to be executioners?

The circumstantial evidence is intriguing rather than damning. One grievance the consorters had against Ray Bennett came from the fact that they provided unofficial security for bookmakers on settling days at the Victorian Club. But, on the day the Bennett gang struck, the usual crew of armed detectives were not there – they had been sent at the last minute on an errand to Frankston, a coincidence that led some to suspect Bennett had connived with a corrupt senior officer to set up the robbery.

One slip during the robbery probably sowed the seeds of the gang's destruction. When the masked men ordered all present to lie face down, one said to the then well-known boxing trainer Ambrose Palmer, 'You too, Ambrose.'

The robber instantly regretted his half-friendly warning. He had once trained at Palmer's gymnasium and knew the old man would recognise his voice. Palmer naturally forgot to mention this to police, the story goes, but accidentally let slip the robber's identity to people connected with the Kane brothers. Word got around, and members of Bennett's gang became targets for opportunists who wanted a share of the bookies' cash.

It was an ideal scenario for gang warfare. War was declared in a Richmond hotel in mid-1978, when Vincent Mikkelsen – a friend of Bennett's – refused a drink from Brian Kane.

Mikkelsen committed an even graver social indiscretion by winning the resulting fight – and biting off part of Kane's ear in the process.

Musing much later about Kane's reaction to this humiliating disfigurement, Joe Gullaci said: 'It's hard to be the number one standover man in town when you've got a piece bitten out of your ear.'

That mouthful of ear was eventually to give Melbourne's underworld heartburn and put the wind up the police force. But all Brian Kane knew then was that it was bad for his reputation – and that wasn't good for business.

Mikkelsen came to expect massive retaliation. Bennett suggested Mikkelsen's life be spared, and was warned: 'If you stick your head in, it will be blown off.'

From there, the story unfolds with brutal inevitability. Fearing a pre-emptive strike, Brian Kane's brother Les – regarded as the most dangerous brother – moved his second wife, Judy, and their family from the western suburbs to a unit in Wantirna, in the far outer-eastern suburbs.

It was a long way from their normal stamping grounds, but not far enough. On 19 October, 1978, a Thursday night, Les and Judy Kane got home to find three masked men waiting. They shoved Judy Kane into a bedroom and her husband into the bathroom, where they shot him with silenced 'machine guns' that, the story goes, had originally been specially modified for the dreaded 'toecutter' Linus Driscoll. This was ironic, considering persistent unsourced suggestions later that Driscoll took the contract to kill Bennett.

The killers threw Kane's body in the boot of his distinctive pink Ford Futura sedan and drove off. Neither the body nor the car were ever found. They had a head start because Judy Kane observed painter and docker protocol by not speaking to police until they heard about her husband's 'disappearance' and contacted her first. Bennett told police, straight-faced, that he'd taken a call on the night of Les Kane's death to say that Kane had 'gone off' and he'd immediately gone into hiding, fearing reprisals.

He wasn't the only one to fear reprisals. When the case went to trial at the Supreme Court in September, 1979, court security measures were extraordinary. There were armed police, marksmen posted outside, and stringent identity and weapon checks on everyone who entered court. Even a prison chaplain, Peter Alexander, was not allowed to visit Bennett.

The three were acquitted, mainly because of the absence of a body. Though pleased with the result, they suspected not everyone was convinced of their innocence. Mikkelsen and Prendergast left Melbourne immediately for distant destinations. (Prendergast was later to make the mistake of returning. He drove a Volvo, but it didn't keep him safe. His body, like Les Kane's, was never found.) And Bennett, still to face charges on the payroll robbery, chose to stay in custody.

Seven weeks later, he was sent to the Magistrates Court for committal. This time, oddly enough, there was no security at all.

So who killed him? And how did he get away with it so easily?

The brief inquest that was theoretically supposed to answer that when it finally sat, raised more questions than answers.

Despite the public interest, and the time available to prepare the brief, it was a slight document – barely a morsel for the eminent legal talent gathered around the bar table.

Joe Gullaci could not represent Gail Bennett and her family because he had been called as a witness. Instead, she hired a prominent criminal barrister, Jack Lazarus.

Lazarus was aggressive but, on instructions, was not out to lay blame in ways that might fan hostilities and make life hard for the widow and her schoolboy son, Danny. Peter Alexander, the knockabout priest who buried Bennett, told the authors that

Lazarus's brief was to defend Bennett's reputation for the sake of his son – not to lead a murder investigation.

With Lazarus choosing his punches carefully, no-one else was swinging wildly, either. The result was a predictably thin account of facts already run in the media – except for one thing.

The brilliant advocate representing the police – John Phillips, QC, later to become Chief Justice – was forced to air rumours claiming that two detectives were implicated in the murder. Given that Lazarus didn't directly accuse anyone, it was the only way that Phillips could try to put such rumours to rest.

The men Phillips named, albeit gently, were Paul John Strang and Brian Francis Murphy.

Strang, a popular consorting squad detective later dismissed over a minor matter, was one of the three detectives supposed to be escorting Bennett, but happened not to be standing near him when the shots were fired.

Murphy, then with the new Metropolitan Regional Crime squad – nicknamed 'Murphy's Marauders' – had no official reason to be at the magistrates court the day Bennett was killed. He arrived from his North Fitzroy office after the shooting, and said later he'd thought the activity outside the court was a demonstration. Extraordinarily, although named at the inquest as a rumoured suspect, Murphy was never interviewed nor called to give evidence. It was that sort of inquiry. Underworld murders are rarely solved, and this never looked like being the exception.

Even the counsel assisting the Coroner submitted there was no evidence the police knew of threats to Bennett beforehand, and blamed the media for airing matters 'improperly put in court and never substantiated.' So solicitous was he about the perception of unfairness to the police involved that the police's own QC was scarcely able to lay it on any thicker. He claimed it had been a bumper week for rubbishing the police, and called on the media to give full coverage if the Coroner found that Murphy and Strang were not involved in the shooting.

Which, of course, is what the Coroner did. But not even he, a policeman's son, could swallow his own assisting counsel's preposterous suggestions that the police didn't know beforehand of any threats to Bennett's safety.

While the Coroner found who didn't do it, he didn't get close to naming who did. But time has loosened tongues. Several detectives involved in the case suggest independently that they've always believed the gunman was Brian Kane, who killed not for money but to avenge the death of his brother, Les. But, they say, it would be extremely unlikely that a criminal as well-known as Kane was, could prowl the court precinct to set up his escape route.

One former detective says matter-of-factly that two former colleagues removed four roofing nails and levered open the tin fence escape route days earlier. Interestingly, an RMIT gardener recalled seeing a man dressed in new overalls and digging with a new garden trowel next to the fence at 6.45am the week before the murder – possibly on the morning of the Melbourne Cup public holiday when the area would have been almost deserted.

The truth, perhaps, went to the grave with Brian Kane, who was shot dead in the Quarry Hotel in Brunswick in November, 1982, almost three years to the day after Bennett's death.

Twenty years on, Brian Murphy was on a short motoring holiday with his wife in Tasmania when contacted by the authors. He said he remembered distinctly the events of late 1979.

So who was the bearded hitman?

'It was Brian,' he said. 'But not this one.'

The strange thing, he added, was that he'd seen a man who looked very like Brian Kane in Lygon Street the night before, and noticed he had grown a beard.

CHAPTER 3

Little Big Man

'What's the problem — run out of bullets?'

DRUG dealing was good to Tom Scarborough. It gave him money, shares, a luxury car and 'Barbie Doll' girlfriends, but it couldn't give him what he craved most ... respect.

He arrived in Melbourne in 1996 and soon became a prodigious heroin distributor, working his way up from street dealer to influential middleman.

When he first started selling heroin in Melbourne he concentrated on servicing street junkies around the Spencer Street railway station and became known as a dealer who was never short of drugs. 'He seemed to have an endless supply,' a girlfriend and sometime customer would later recall.

In the beginning he lived in a modest city hotel but as he climbed the drug dealing ladder he moved to luxury serviced apartments and five star hotels. Money was not a problem and he bragged to friends he was making $7000 a week.

The dealer had grown up in Adelaide after arriving from Vietnam in 1981. Then he was known as Kuong Pham, but he changed his name to Tom Scarborough, taking the surname of a girl who had become an obsession to the little man with the big ideas.

The 163-centimetre Scarborough was attracted to power and control but he lacked the presence to be an authority figure. 'I wanted to join the police force at eighteen but I was too fat,' he was to reveal.

'JANE' was a pretty young woman in the advertising industry who lived in middle Melbourne with her family. But, like too many of her generation, she had a secret, a heroin habit requiring her to buy a thirty-dollar cap every day.

As a small-time user, she had to take her luck buying on the street, trying to find dealers whenever she wanted to score. In December, 1996, she went to the Richmond railway station and saw a man she instinctively knew was just like her. She went to him and asked if she could wait and buy from his dealer. He had no problem as long as he went first.

Jane bought from the small Asian man who arrived a few minutes later. She went straight to the toilet to inject. After the rush she walked back to the dealer, who introduced himself as Tom.

Jane and her new friend went for a drink in a city bar and began a relationship. Years later she is blunt about the mutual attraction: 'I wanted the heroin and Tom wanted sex.'

She moved in with him – first at a Brunswick apartment that included maid service. Tom was busy selling heroin to at least thirty people a day, with each deal being between fifty and three hundred dollars.

In between deals the dealer doted on her, providing her with a gram of heroin a day – although he wanted her to stop. 'At times he would try and with-hold it from me but eventually he would give it to me. He always had plenty of heroin.'

He put money in her bank account and made sure she wanted for nothing. 'At times we would go shopping together and buy clothes. We would spend up to a couple of thousand dollars between us. I would go the hairdressers three times a week, which would cost at least fifty dollars a time. I would go to the solarium at least three times a week, which was twenty dollars each time.

'Money was never a problem because, no matter what the cost was, Tom was always able to cover it.'

He would leave the apartment and return with a rock of heroin about the size of a golf ball. He would use a credit card to cut it into foils to sell.

They moved every few weeks through South Yarra and Prahran and St Kilda. If she liked the look of a coat she would pretend to think it was too expensive, knowing he would peel off a roll of notes and buy it for her.

They rarely went out in the conventional sense, apart from shopping trips. 'Our life was fairly mundane. We didn't do a lot. We would go and buy clothes at least once a week and I had had very expensive tastes because Tom was always paying for it. He never told me that I couldn't have something.'

Finally Jane decided to get control of her life. She waited until Scarborough was out selling heroin, then flew to Sydney and a pre-booked detox clinic.

As with most junkies, her first attempt to clean-up failed and she rang her dealer boyfriend, who flew to Sydney to get her. It was then she saw another side to him. 'Tom said if I ever left him again without telling him he would kill my family.'

But she did escape a few weeks later and although he hired a private detective to find her, she had finally broken the golden chain. 'I have not used heroin since I left Tom,' Jane said.

If Scarborough was heartbroken, he hid it well and was soon out hunting a replacement. He was a regular at Melbourne strip clubs and was popular with the girls with his cheeky smile and wad of money.

He would sip Coke or water and tip the waitresses with $100 notes. He then found what he was looking for – a girl he described as a 'tall, blonde Barbie Doll.'

She worked at the Men's Gallery table dancing venue and also managed a clothing store in Richmond. Scarborough believed the quickest way to her heart was through a heroin-filled syringe.

Twice a week he would go to the shop and give 'Karen' free heroin. 'He would give me eight to ten caps to last me a few days.'

Strangely, while he would provide her with heroin he would lecture her to give up the drugs. He finally offered her $5000 to give up and booked her into an expensive clinic in March, 1998.

He would ring her every day, shower her with gifts, pay her rent and cover expensive car repairs. He even paid $7000 cash for her breast implant surgery.

The young woman claimed they were 'just friends,' although she admitted 'he was totally obsessed by me.'

The drug dealer who wanted to be a big man didn't want to be 'just friends'. He wanted to be feared and his attitude started to change as he began to talk like a gangster. 'I thought he was pretending to be a bad boy,' Karen said.

He started to acquire the tools of the tough guy trade, including a .357 magnum pistol, a .32 revolver and a police extendable baton. He also tried to buy automatic military weapons 'like the ones used by Julian Knight in Hoddle Street.'

To complete his crime-boss fantasy he needed a Hollywood-style fast car. He bought a high powered Toyota Lexus SC 4000 sports car for $51,444 on 6 January, 1999. It was his ultimate toy and Scarborough was to brag: 'Nothing can beat it, except for a F50 Ferrari and a Lamborghini.'

LITTLE BIG MAN

No-one is sure what made Tom Scarborough unravel, and if anyone does suspect they're not talking about it. But something tipped the little man with the guns and the fast car over the edge in February, 1999, and for six days he drove around Melbourne shooting at anyone or anything that annoyed him until he was shot in a gun battle with police. But the incident that began it all was so trivial it almost defies description.

A man on his way to work didn't bother to move out of the fast lane on a busy Melbourne road. It was enough to drive the little man with the big ego out of his mind.

It happened at 11.05am, 17 February, on the Nepean Highway in East Brighton.

LOU PICCININ, a self-employed plumber, was driving his white Toyota van along the busy highway. He was in the far right lane of the four-lane road travelling on the speed limit of 80kmh when he heard the driver behind him repeatedly sounding his horn.

He glanced in his rear-view mirror to see the driver of a dark green Lexus with tinted windows swerve over two lanes of traffic then swing back to the middle lane, cutting off Reginald Nankervis, a local motor mechanic who was late for an appointment with his solicitor.

Nankervis was in no mood to tolerate fools on the road and when he was cut off by the sports car he yelled out, 'You idiot!'

Unfortunately, the man at the wheel of the Lexus was not one to turn the other cheek. He was armed and unbalanced.

Nankervis saw the face of the driver in the sports car's external mirror mouthing words back. Most road rage incidents go no further than that, but this was no normal intolerant driver. If the next set of lights had been green nothing may have happened, but they were red and the traffic stopped.

Scarborough got out of his car, grabbed an extendable baton, and started towards Nankervis. 'I thought that I was really in trouble.' But Scarborough turned to the left and began to attack Piccinin's van, also pulled up at the lights. He smashed in the rear window with the baton.

He then asked what appeared to him to be a simple question. 'Didn't you hear me beeping for you to get out of the way?'

Piccinin replied, 'The speed limit's 80 kilometres an hour – what do you want me to do?

'He was an imbecile and I couldn't talk to him,' Piccinin later told police. He didn't seem to grasp there was no value in arguing with a man who is beating your van with an iron bar.

But a large man in a furniture truck managed to break up the confrontation. The driver, Steve, told police 'I thought he was going to hit him for sure so I yelled out, "get back in your f...... car".'

The passenger in the furniture truck said of this: 'I got the feeling that he (Scarborough) shit himself … Steve is a big, mean-looking guy.'

Piccinin had to jump out of the way when Scarborough sped off. The shaken plumber drove straight to the Moorabbin police station to report the incident.

A policewoman on duty took the details and was quickly able to find Scarborough's mobile phone number. She rang and left a message and the suspect obligingly rang back a few minutes later.

Scarborough was surprisingly co-operative – he cheerfully admitted the road rage incident, but claimed Piccinin 'thought he was king of the road.'

When the policewoman asked him to come to the station he refused. 'I can't be bothered – good luck finding me.'

He then hung up only to ring back and say, 'I think you're a lesbo with a power trip and a gun.' He was running off the rails.

LITTLE BIG MAN

February 19, 5.50 pm. Jam Factory, South Yarra: A young cinema worker had just finished work at the Village Centre at the Jam Factory and had walked to the car park to drive home when she saw a man unscrewing the number plates from a car.

A co-worker, Gino Munari, was also there, having slipped out for a cigarette. He believed the car was owned by a fellow member of staff so he approached the man and asked him what he was doing.

Tom Scarborough tried to bluff his way out of trouble, claiming the car was owned by a friend. Munari said he didn't believe him, but Scarborough continued to work on the plates.

As he walked off with the number plates he said, 'I hate f...... heroes.'

He was later to use the plates on his sports car.

February 21: It was around 6am, a Sunday, when Tom Scarborough went to the Viper Room in Prahran to meet Nicole, a dancer from the Men's Gallery.

He told her, 'I am not going to take this shit any more ... If they take me down I'm going to make sure I go down in a blaze of bullets like Julian Knight ... They won't catch me in my car.'

He said he was carrying a gun and a baton and swore 'No more Mister Nice Guy.'

Scarborough said if the bouncer had not let him in he would have attacked him with the baton.

The girl knew the chubby little man and thought his tough talk was fake. 'I did not believe what Tom was saying. I thought he was just bragging and trying to impress me.'

By the next day she knew she was wrong.

PHONG DUI NGUYEN was a small-time heroin dealer who used to siphon small amounts of drugs from his sales to feed his own habit.

When Scarborough came to Melbourne in 1996 Nguyen was his supplier but within twelve months the roles had been reversed. 'Tom started to get bigger and bigger,' Nguyen was to say later. By early 1999 Nguyen was $1600 in debt to his former customer.

It was nearly midnight when Nguyen, his girlfriend, May Tran, and another friend, Ha Vu, sat in a car listening to the radio in the driveway of a house in Gray Street, Yarraville.

'The driver's side window was open because it was a warm night. 'We just continued to talk, figuring where to go,' Nguyen said.

May Tran heard a noise and said, 'There is someone outside.' Nguyen opened the car door and put his right foot on the driveway when he spotted Scarborough, who was carrying a handgun. 'He then fired a shot and it hit me in the chest.'

He didn't stop there – hitting the wounded man with a total of six shots from his .357 magnum. 'I tossed my body around to try to protect myself, but he kept firing the gun into my body.'

The next thing the injured man saw was his mother crying and he told her 'I'm dying.' But he wasn't, despite being shot in the chest, leg and arm.

When police later asked Scarborough why he shot Nguyen he said, 'He's basically a double crosser.'

February 22, 1999: Frank Borrello was driving his zippy little soft top along Munro Street, Coburg, around lunchtime when he had to veer around the nose of a big green sports car doing a left hand turn into the same street, just in front of him.

He could hear the driver of the sports car sounding his horn and flashing his lights behind him. 'I thought that this person might have known me and recognised my car.'

He was wrong.

Borrello stopped at the corner of Munro Street and Sydney

Road and the green car pulled up beside him. Scarborough started to abuse the driver. 'You f...... wanker,' he said before firing one shot into the car. Borrello thought it was a cap gun. Only later, when he found the neat bullet hole just above the petrol tank, did he realise what a close shave he'd had.

That night Scarborough went back to Men's Gallery to meet Nicole. The bouncer on the door told him not to annoy the staff. What the crowd controller didn't know was that the small, smiling patron was out of control. 'If he (the bouncer) wasn't going to let me in I was going to pop him at the front door,' Scarborough boasted later, and there is no reason to believe he didn't mean it.

He was laughing when he said to Nicole, 'I told you I won't get walked on again.'

He started bragging about shooting Nguyen. 'He deserved it. I emptied the whole gun on him and all he could say was, "sorry mate".'

February 23, 1999: Christopher Dunn had dropped his girlfriend off at work in Carlton and was heading to see a friend in Hawthorn when he noticed a driver in a dark sports car wanting to veer right to avoid parked cars.

Dunn had to stop for a tram in Riversdale Road, Hawthorn, so he tooted his horn to tell the other driver he could slip in front of him. It was a big mistake.

The driver was Tom Scarborough, who was looking for any excuse to shoot at people. Dunn, twenty six, saw the driver in front of him angrily waving his arms about.

Dunn pulled up behind the car at a set of lights and noticed the driver 'flipped him the bird' – giving him the one-finger salute.

At the next set of lights Dunn pulled up on the left of the angry driver and made his next mistake. Through the open window he yelled – 'What's your problem? Get over it.' Scarborough pulled out his gun and started blasting Dunn's car.

The lights changed but Dunn was caught in heavy traffic and couldn't escape. 'He continued to fire the gun at me. I heard the gun "click".'

Dunn believed the gun was empty. Then he did something beyond belief. He began to taunt the man who had just tried to kill him. 'What's the problem (expletive deleted) – run out of bullets?' he asked.

He assumed that the madman next to him only had one gun. It was a mistake, and nearly a fatal one.

Scarborough might have emptied one gun, but he had another one, a bigger one, the .357 magnum.

Dunn headed up the driveway of his friend's home as Scarborough followed, trying to blast him again. Dunn was lucky Scarborough was a bad shot. One bullet just grazed his stomach and arm. He was a few centimetres from death.

Police were later to establish that Dunn's car was hit with nine shots – six .32 slugs and three from the magnum.

Scarborough later told police: 'We both started arguing and I basically wanted to scare him.' He said that after he had emptied the gun the man taunted him by saying 'Run out of bullets have you, dickhead?'

'I took out my .357 and pumped three more rounds into him. I thought this guy had guts so I thought I'll give him a couple. He was a real road rager, man.'

LATER that day Scarborough went to Karen's flat in Hawthorn. He was supposed to take her shopping for a car.

Karen saw the little drug dealer as a soft touch but the cheerful man with the fat wallet had changed. He turned savage. 'He was calling me "slut" and told me to shut up.' He went into the bathroom with his two guns in a black bag and reloaded them. Stupidly, Karen decided to go ahead with the shopping trip with this disturbed, violent and armed drug dealer. 'He told me it was at my own risk if I get in the car and that I was taking a risk by hopping in the car. He told me if any police pulls him over he was going to shoot them. I didn't believe him.'

She had to stay in the back seat of the two-door sports car. He had a new obsession in the front seat – his guns.

SENIOR CONSTABLE Jason Striegher was stationed at the Epping Traffic Operations Group and was rostered to work a 7am to 3pm that day.

He followed his usual routine of grabbing his utility belt, handcuffs, extendable baton, capsicum spray and six-shot Smith & Wesson revolver. He looked at the pistol and read the serial number before writing down the last three digits – 903 – in the station registry.

He collected his equipment box containing a street directory, portable radio, penalty notice books, preliminary breath test kit and traffic equipment. There was one other item in the box – a ballistic vest.

After finishing some paper work he walked out to his unmarked white Ford about 8.30am to begin the day's patrols.

He put his equipment box on the front passenger seat and opened the boot to put the cumbersome vest in a special carrier fitted in the car.

The dayshift patrol, unlike the afternoon and night shift, usually work alone, or in police terminology – 'one-up'.

Jason Striegher was not worried, he knew from experience there was little danger to traffic police in busy Melbourne during the middle of the day.

But the events of the next few hours were to show that police were always in danger and that even a routine traffic patrol could not be taken for granted. It began as a normal shift on a normal day. At mid-morning, while out on the road, he heard a police broadcast to all units to look for a suspect's car believed to have been involved in shooting incidents.

He jotted down the registration number on his left hand.

One of the advantages of working in the Epping district was that Striegher lived close by. Around 11.40am he popped home to make some sandwiches. He took his portable radio with him and heard a broadcast that indicated the wanted car was heading his way.

He drove down Rosanna Road and saw the green sports car being followed by a marked police car. The traffic cop turned on his flashing lights and siren and U-turned to fall in behind.

The marked car passed the Lexus and the sports car pulled over.

Senior Constable Striegher jumped from his car. His ballistic vest was still in its secure holder locked in the boot. It was far too late to grab it.

By the time Striegher was opening his car door Scarborough was already on the move with a gun in his hand. He said to Karen, who was still in the back seat, 'This is it. It's all over.'

He raised his .357 magnum towards the policeman. Striegher unclipped his holster and started to draw his service revolver, shouting 'he's got a gun.'

Police say that in a gunfight with handguns most shots miss the mark. Even though Scarborough was pointing the gun at the policeman the odds were still that he would miss. But he didn't. Senior Constable Striegher was hit in the chest with the very first shot. The bullet entered the left side of his chest and burst out the other side. 'I thought I was going to be killed.'

Even though he was seriously injured Striegher responded as he had been trained. He did not turn and run, he kept his eyes on the gunman and moved back, using his police car as cover.

But Scarborough clearly wanted to finish the injured man. 'I could see him moving towards me. He was walking, he was also dodging and weaving from side to side. He had both of his arms fully extended in front of him, holding the firearm with both hands.

'As he was walking towards me I fired one or two shots at this person.'

The policeman couldn't take a two-handed stance to fire. He had to use his left arm to hold his wounded chest and stuck a finger in the exit wound to staunch the blood.

Scarborough was clearly trying to finish the wounded man. It was later described as like 'stalking prey.' He kept coming and fired two more shots. 'It looked to me as if he was chasing me trying to get into a position to get a better shot at me,' the injured policeman was to say.

Striegher was fighting for his life as blood seeped from his wounds, but despite severe internal injuries he fired at least another two shots.

It was like a movie scene. The men kept firing at each other and Striegher thought they both must be close to being out of ammunition.

He then heard a shot from his left and saw Scarborough turn and fire twice more. Striegher had one shot left and he wanted to make it count. He bent down and used the boot of his car to steady his arm. He fired from about four metres. To this day he doesn't know if it hit the gunman.

Out of ammunition, he moved to the side of his police car and ducked for cover. He was trying to use his speed-loader to reload but he still had to use his left arm to hold his wound.

He then heard another policeman yell 'He's down!'

SERGEANT Simon Delaney was at the Heidelberg station when he heard a police radio broadcast that there had been a shooting incident involving the driver of a dark coupe. He made a mental note but it was not a matter to concern him. 'There was no suggestion that there was any connection between this vehicle and my area.'

But, just after midday, police in the station were told the car had been spotted on the Eastern Freeway heading towards them.

The divisional van with two uniformed police and an unmarked car with four detectives left the station to try and intercept the gunman. Delaney also jumped in a marked car to join the search.

He was at the corner of Burgundy Street and Rosanna Road when he saw the suspect car go past. He followed along Rosanna Road and when the car began to slow he slipped in front and stopped at an angle to block the possibility of a U-turn escape.

Delaney saw Scarborough jump from the Lexus and raise his gun. The sergeant used his car as a shield and drew his revolver.

He could see the gunman focus and fire at Senior Constable Striegher. He watched the man stalk Striegher, then he saw him turn and point the gun at him.

'I had absolutely no doubt in my mind that this person was about to kill me. I then fired my revolver at this male and continued firing until he fell to the ground.

'I am not sure how many shots I fired. It was certainly more than two and could have been up to six.' He said the whole incident took only fifteen seconds.

The fact that Scarborough turned on the other policeman almost certainly saved Striegher's life.

The four Heidelberg detectives had been out conducting early morning raids in Reservoir and had already arrested two men that day. They were back in their office when they got a call at 12.10pm with the report that someone had seen a man with a gun in a green Toyota sports car. They all hopped in the station's gold coloured Holden station wagon to try and find him.

The drove straight into the gunfight. Senior Detective Gerard Gaul yelled out 'Police. Don't move!'

'He (Scarborough) continued to fire his firearm at the uniform member. I believed at that instant that if I did not fire my revolver at this offender that the uniform member would be killed.

'I took deliberate aim at this offender and then discharged one round … but I am unable to say if the round struck him or not.

'As soon as I discharged my revolver the offender stopped firing and stopped advancing. The offender appeared unsteady on his feet and staggered backwards a few steps towards his vehicle before slumping on the footpath.'

Senior Detective Michael Hall ran to the wounded gunman. Even though he had been shot, Scarborough still wanted to talk. 'Why don't you finish the job? Why didn't you kill me?' he demanded.

When he was asked his name he said, 'I'm in too much pain to remember.'

Hall kicked the magnum away from the injured man but when Scarborough was searched police found another small, silver handgun in his pocket.

Jason Striegher was wounded on both sides of the chest. When the bullets had hit him it was as if he had been punched and winded, he was to say later.

He could feel the rush of blood from the wounds, then he felt the pain. He was conscious but when he looked up he saw what he described as 'the terror' in the eyes of the colleagues who were helping him. He knew then he was in serious trouble.

Ambulance Officer Anthony Coffey was the first to treat Striegher, who told him he had a burning pain through his chest and was deeply distressed. He ripped the distressed policeman's blood-soaked shirt open to tend to the wounds.

When he was placed in the back of the ambulance, Striegher

didn't want to waste time answering questions. He said, 'Get this old bus moving.'

As ambulance officers worked on the injured gunman at the scene he kept yelling, 'It took four of you to put me down, why don't you finish me off, put a bullet in my head?'

In the emergency room at the Austin Hospital Scarborough would still not shut up. 'Don't help me, I'm scum. Go on, laugh at me. Just shoot me and finish me off. It took four to one, that's fair, four to one.'

He started to chant, 'I won, I won, I did it for fun. Four to one and I won.'

He was shot in the arm and the body. It is still not known which of the three police who fired at him actually hit him. One of the police bullets cannot be tested to see which gun it came from. It remains wedged in one of Scarborough's vertebrae.

If a bullet misses its target it is still potentially lethal. Police found that one bullet from the gunfight went through the window of a nearby unit, piercing a curtain, wall and a shower screen before ending up in the shower.

Another bullet passed through the main bedroom of a house and ended up stuck in a wall. More bullet holes were found in houses and a garage in the area. One travelled three hundred metres down the road. Two police cars crashed as the drivers tried to avoid being exposed to the gun battle.

When Scarborough was out of danger he was interviewed by members of the Asian Squad in the Austin Hospital. He gave his occupation as 'compulsive gambler'.

Even though he knew he would be charged with attempted murder and other serious charges he still wanted to talk about his car. 'A Lexus SC 4000, fully imported. Nothing can beat it, except for a F50 Ferrari and a Lamborghini.'

During his formal interview he was shown a picture of the car. 'Very nice, eh?' he boasted.

MORE than a year after the shooting many of those involved were still suffering flashbacks and nightmares.

Christopher Dunn, the driver who baited Scarborough that he had run out of bullets, delayed his planned return to study at Melbourne University. He became isolated and suffers anxiety when driving, fearing he may be shot.

Seven police involved in the arrest and shooting of Scarborough all reported stress-related problems after the Heidelberg gunfight.

One of the detectives found that when she did any police training involving scenarios with offenders armed with guns she suffered flashbacks. She has since quit the force after fourteen years service.

The policeman who cradled the injured Jason Striegher on the ground at Heidelberg still has difficulty sleeping.

A detective who went to the scene found he was becoming increasingly worried that his policewoman wife, who was pregnant at the time, could be shot while on duty.

Another has had disturbed sleep and is now worried he could be shot. He has started smoking again.

One policeman has yet to rid himself of feelings of self doubts because he did not fire at Scarborough during the gunfight.

Jason Striegher has made a good recovery from his physical wounds (he lost his gall bladder and part of his liver) and is determined to keep a positive outlook to life and his job.

But he doesn't swim or surf as much as he once did because he is self-conscious about the large L-shaped scar on his stomach.

He now wears a light undercover-style ballistic vest when out on patrol. It irritates the scar tissue, reminding him daily of how close he was to death.

Justice Bernie Teague of the Supreme Court decided that the cause of all this, Tom Scarborough, should pay compensation for what he had done. The gunman's assets, including his portfolio of 720 AMP, ten thousand Crown and a thousand Woodside Petroleum shares were seized. Then came the final blow: his fast car was sold for $33,655.

He was left with nothing except a sentence of twenty years with a minimum of fifteen after pleading guilty to three counts of attempted murder and drug trafficking.

EVEN now the question still remains, why did Tom Scarborough declare war on Melbourne?

Was he determined to commit 'suicide by cop?'

While he was lying in his hospital bed a policeman asked him, 'Did you want to die?'

He answered: 'No, everyone wants to live … why would I want to die when I've got a car only a Lamborghini can beat?'

CHAPTER 4

A Sour Apple that Turned Rotten

*The 'lifestyle' was the major crime squad's notorious
work practices — referred to as 'work hard, play hard.'
At least Hicks got it half right.*

FOR an astute and experienced criminal Laurence Joseph
Sumner was beginning to get sloppy. A self-made expert in the
lucrative amphetamines industry, he was to make a mistake
worthy of a novice and would soon pay the price.

Sumner had come to crime relatively late but had proved a
quick and enthusiastic learner. He was rumored to have been
involved in planting a bomb under the car of the Melbourne
Godfather, Liborio Benvenuto, in 1983 and to have provided
the gun used to kill Giuseppe Arena outside his Bayswater
home in 1987.

In 1991 he was on bail over an amphetamines lab when police
learned he was driving a stolen car and was silly enough to park
it at night in the driveway of his double-storey house in
Avondale Heights, an outer-western suburb of Melbourne.

Drug squad detectives went to the house one night to find the
stolen car so they could revoke his bail. As expected, the car
was in the drive. But there was a bonus for the police.

As a drug squad detective, Wayne Strawhorn, walked up the driveway he could hear an industrial pump and see water pouring out of a hose poking from the garage. His experienced nose picked up the odour of amphetamine chemicals through the slightly opened door.

Some drug squad operations can take years of detailed investigation, while others can be laughably easy. This was one of the latter. The police simply walked up, opened the garage, grabbed their man and a truckload of evidence.

In the vernacular Sumner was 'done cold'. The case was watertight and the exhibits were under lock and key – or so the detectives thought.

Sumner was experienced enough to know that even the best lawyer could not save him this time. What he needed was a break, and it came from another serious criminal who said he had information to sell that would destroy the police case.

It is believed Sumner paid several thousand dollars for the red-hot information. He was told to demand that all the drugs seized in his case should be re-tested.

The results, he was assured, might surprise.

CLOSE to Melbourne Airport, off Mickleham Road, police have a property, known as Attwood, used for training dogs and horses and to teach high-speed driving techniques. But, in 1988, speed of a different sort found its way to Attwood. That year police had to find a place to store volatile chemicals – such as used to make amphetamines – well away from populated areas. The training area at Attwood was considered, if not ideal, at least adequate.

Seized drugs were first tested at the Forensic Science Laboratory and then transported to Attwood where they were kept in six old, locked shipping containers.

The keys were kept in the drug squad where they were

supposed to be safe. The man in charge of them was Senior Detective Kevin Hicks, a former major crime squad detective. Indeed, Hicks bought new locks and keys in April, 1992, allegedly to improve security.

When Sumner's lawyer called for the drugs to be re-analysed the prosecution thought it was, at best, just a shot in the dark, but it proved to be perfectly aimed.

What was found to be sitting in drums and containers in Attwood bore no resemblance to the materials tested earlier by Forensic Science.

Containers filled with methylamphetamine had mysteriously turned into Coca Cola.

Ten kilograms of an ingredient used in the manufacture of speed, red phosphorous, had been replaced with red tile grout. Puzzlingly, the locks were secure and there were no signs of a break-in.

It was an inside job.

In June, 1992, police launched an internal inquiry to find out who switched the drugs. They found a glove impression on one of the exhibits which suggested a burglary had taken place, but they could not find if the drugs had been switched at the Forensic Science Laboratory or Attwood.

Despite the finding Sumner was found guilty based on the original analysis. But it would take another eight years to prove who was the traitor in the camp.

AROUND the time police realised they were being sold out from within a young detective received a message at the drug squad that would change his life and put him in the uncomfortable role of whistle blower.

Lachlan McCulloch was not a detective of the old school. But the former private schoolboy who had drifted into policing found he had a real flair for catching criminals.

An accomplished undercover operative, he was to infiltrate the infamous Pettingill drug family as a yuppie who wanted drugs to sell to his friends on the ski slopes. His work resulted in the arrest of Kath Pettingill and her son, Trevor.

The job had not yet worn McCulloch down, although he had seen more than his share of action. He was commended for bravery when he saved a child from a dangerous and mentally unbalanced man in September, 1990, and had seen a colleague shoot a man dead in front of him in St Kilda.

But, to McCulloch, the drug squad was the pinnacle of his career. It would also prove to be his undoing.

The message he received on 8 April, 1992, was from the warehouse manager at a chemical supply company. The manager was suspicious over a series of purchases of chemicals and laboratory equipment made over the previous five weeks.

McCulloch went out to the Mulgrave company and asked for the dockets. It took only a quick scan confirmed his suspicions. Whoever was buying the gear was setting up an amphetamines lab.

The salesman at the front counter was able to give a detailed description of the James Sweetin, the man buying the equipment. More than that, he was able to slip out and jot down the man's car number.

It was a maroon Subaru station wagon registered to a nondescript company. Further investigations found the car had recently been pulled over by police on a routine traffic check. The driver was Peter Pilaranos, whose name meant nothing to McCulloch at the time.

Although the two men had not met, this was to be a pivotal moment in their lives. In a strange way, it would consume both of them and cost them their careers.

McCulloch returned to his office and briefed his sergeant, who considered there was sufficient information to justify an immediate investigation, code-named Cane. The trail led to Pilarinos's huge home, set on three large blocks in the eastern suburb of Doncaster.

At 4.35am on 13 July, 1992, McCulloch went through the garbage in the wheelie bin left outside and found a ripped up note in an empty dog food tin.

He stuck it together and saw it was an amphetamines recipe with prices next to the chemicals. But next to methylamine was the value of $0.00.

Later, police were to find Pilarinos didn't need to pay for methalymine because he had stolen it from the Attwood storage dump. His only cost was to pay off Hicks.

Police started to monitor James Sweetin's phone at his house in Ferntree Gully. They expected it would be a text book operation.

But on 29 September Sweetin told a drug associate, Ken Milton, on the telephone that he was about to find out if the line was tapped. When he rang back he was in no doubt. 'Don't say my name, treat your rear vision mirrors like guardian angels, treat this thing like everybody is listening.'

Police secretly broke into the gang's amphetamines lab in Ferntree Gully next day. It had already been packed up into storage boxes. McCulloch knew he had been sold out and Operation Cane was terminated.

Some police are able to shrug their shoulders at corruption. Lachlan McCulloch was not one of them. He started a one-man war against Pilarinos that would last years.

He launched Operation Austin in 1995 but, again, Pilarinos was warned off. In 1996 he worked on Operation Redalen which resulted in Sweetin being caught at a lab.

Finally, Sweetin confessed to McCulloch who had sold him out during Operation Cane.

It was Kevin Hicks.

SOMETIMES the police who go bad are high-flyers. Such as the notorious former NSW detective, Roger Rogerson, who helped solve some of Australia's most baffling crimes before being exposed as bent. Police like Rogerson tend to be brave to the point of recklessness and appear to live for their job before they turn bad.

But Kevin Hicks was not that type – he was a plodder, and a lazy one at that.

He was twenty years old when he left his hometown of Hamilton in Victoria's western district to join the police force in Melbourne in 1974. For a big country lad it offered security. You faced the sack only if you were crooked and caught red handed, as he was to find from his own bitter experience.

In the sixth squad trained in 1974 Hicks was middle of the road and showed no signs of being highly motivated or highly involved. His first eight years on the road did nothing to suggest he would be a late bloomer or a charismatic leader.

So it was a surprise when he put in for the tough major crime squad in the early 1980s, and an even bigger one that he was accepted. He was to become involved in hunting some of the country's most dangerous men, including Pavel Marinoff – 'Mad Max' – the man who shot six police in 1985-1986. He was seen as brave enough but by no means a star investigator.

'He was a naive country lad. He was a good bloke but not a real hard worker,' a former major crime squad detective said.

'He sort of just fell into the lifestyle.'

The 'lifestyle' was the major crime squad's notorious work practices – referred to euphemistically as 'work hard, play hard.' At least Hicks got it half right.

With his curly hair and round face he became known as 'Koala Bear' because there were already detectives nicknamed Bear and Polar Bear in the squad.

A former major crime squad detective, Peter Spence, who

was to give character evidence for Hicks in court, said that after chasing some of the state's most dangerous criminals squad detectives would sometimes go to 'lunch' and drink until 5am the next day.

Another colleague said Hicks eventually found work to be a tiresome distraction from drinking.

One of the duties of the major crime squad was to host police from around the country who would descend on Melbourne during the Cup Carnival each spring.

Officially, this was to log the movements of gangsters who went to the races. Unofficially, it was an excuse to binge drink for weeks.

'For about a month a year we were called the Ghurkas because we took no prisoners,' one was to recall.

Added to this was constant visits from detectives who expected to be taken out on the town. Many in the squad tired of the constant drinking and wanted to catch crooks. Hicks wasn't one of them. He was, rather, a crook who was tired of occasionally working and wanted to catch another drink.

While he was the longest serving member of the squad he had long since stopped being productive. He was made unofficial social secretary and his full time duties largely revolved around entertaining squad guests and 'getting on the piss.'

He became lethargic and withdrawn but he didn't seek, nor was offered, counselling. According to Spence, Hicks' marriage broke up because of his lifestyle.

His police diary would show 'licensing duties' nearly every third day – a code for pub crawls. His arrest record was lamentable. He made only one arrest in almost two years and, despite repeated warnings, he refused to lift his work rate.

The major crime squad was running out of control. It had a squad lunch in an outer-suburban hotel that ended in chaos after a drunken detective began to head-butt members of the public in the men's toilet. There were further arguments because the detectives believed the meal should be free, despite the protests of the licensee.

By late 1991 it was all too much, or too little.

Hicks was sacked from the 'majors' and moved to the drug squad as assistant property steward in January, 1992. For an operational detective it seemed a massive slap in the face to be made a clerk to keep him out of mischief.

In reality, he was given the keys to the lolly shop.

MOST detectives knew Hicksy. They all drank in the police club or the old City Court Hotel. He was seen as rock solid, quiet but staunch.

Most thought he had been shafted by being moved from the major crime squad and everyone in the drug squad tried to help him recover his collapsed self esteem.

'He was a lost soul. I thought he was like a big, dumb teddy bear,' observed a detective who worked at the drug squad at the time.

'He would come downstairs with his mug of coffee and go from crew to crew for a chat. We all talked to him about our jobs because we thought he missed the action. Now we know he was selling us out.'

While no-one suspected the affable property steward there were clear problems in the drug squad. A surveillance photo of Sweetin that McCulloch had stuck on his locker was stolen.

Promising jobs would turn cold and some targets seemed uncannily able to anticipate police actions.

In 1993 Australia's biggest amphetamines manufacturer, John William Samuel Higgs, was preparing for a big 'cook' but he cancelled it suddenly, telling his subordinates he knew that police were about to launch a blitz.

In a major drug investigation, code-named Operation

Pipeline, an undercover policeman was at the point of buying three machine guns when his target went cold. The criminal moved to Sydney and would not deal with the undercover. It was clear the job had been sold out from within.

There were a series of internal investigations but the rat in the ranks was not uncovered.

Meanwhile Kevin Hicks, the devastated major crime squad detective, was making a comeback of sorts. He seemed to be taking his job quite seriously.

When he arrived at the squad Hicks had been struggling with alimony payments, as his marriage had broken up three years years earlier. In police circles his battered 1975 Ford station wagon was a standing joke, often sitting in the no-standing zone outside the old watch-house in Russell Street for up to a week because he could not afford to fill the tank.

But he was to buy a Mitsubishi V6 four-wheel-drive and a top class motorcycle and took his girlfriend to Disneyland, Hawaii and California for eight weeks on an expensive holiday.

He bought into a racehorse and seemed to be doing well on the punt. Fellow police, suspicious of almost everyone except one of their own colleagues, apparently thought his luck had changed and he was getting his life back together.

Not for a moment did they think the quiet man was talking to the wrong people. If anyone suspected the truth, they weren't sharing it.

Hicks, meanwhile, was looting the containers he was paid to protect, recycling the drugs and chemicals seized by his drug squad mates that he chatted with every day. He was selling out jobs, risking the lives of undercover police and informers.

Years in the major crime squad had given Hicks an impressive network of criminal contacts. One of those was Peter Pilarinos, a dangerous criminal with ambitions to be a crime boss. Many detectives knew the Pilarinos family well and some of the serious crime squads held their social nights at a nightclub owned by his brother. Some detectives had worked the door as a part-time job.

But most detectives saw Peter for what he was: a manipulator with no scruples. 'He is an arrogant bastard who believed he was invincible,' one detective said.

In early 1992, Pilarinos wanted to manufacture amphetamines. His cook, James Sweetin, said they would have trouble finding the vital ingredient – methylamine – but Pilarinos said he had a tame copper who could provide what they needed.

Hicks met Pilarinos in the Aegean Restaurant in Brunswick Street, Fitzroy. No-one needed to sell the idea to Hicks. He was quite prepared to hand over the keys to the compound to and describe where the chemicals were sorted.

Pilarinos, Sweetin and Milton drove to Attwood and parked away from the compound. Wearing gloves and using keys provided by Hicks they were able to take 150 litres of methylamine without any problem.

They returned again and again to steal more chemicals, replacing the liquid with Coca Cola and red phosphorous with tile grout.

But Hicks did more than just provide keys. He stole phenylacetic from the compound and dropped it off in a rubbish bin at a sports ground near Attwood. And there were allegations, although never proven, that he stole truckloads of seized cannabis that should have been destroyed and sold it back through Pilarinos. The gang even stole chemical text books from the lock-up to ensure they were producing speed of the highest quality by the latest methods.

Hicks kept them up to date on the state of any investigation into his group and tipped them off that police planned to put a secret video camera outside Pilarinos's home in Doncaster and had Sweetin's home under surveillance.

He even told Pilarinos of the evidence gathered by Lachlan McCulloch on his early-morning garbage run.

The gang needed ketone to make a batch of amphetamines and Pilarinos ordered six litres for $12,000 from an unemployed criminal who owned a sixty-square home in Yarra Glen.

When it was delivered to a Doncaster house, Hicks staged a fake raid using a bodgy firearms warrant. He gave one of the crooks present a clip over the ear and threatened to arrest all present.

The man who delivered the drugs was allowed to leave. The chemicals weren't.

No-one asked why one detective in a station wagon was conducting raids. They knew they were being ripped off – but who do amphetamines dealers complain to?

PILARINOS did something that a succession of senior police failed to do. He actually got Hicks to work.

But the former major crime squad failure didn't come cheap. Once, before he was about to take his girlfriend to the US in 1993 he demanded extra money for travel expenses.

Pilarinos and another man met him on a footbridge in Glen Iris and gave him an envelope with cash. Records show that Hicks and his girlfriend left for the US on 3 May that year for an eight-week luxury holiday.

Pilarinos was pleasant enough to his tame copper when they met, often at the Aegean Restaurant, but behind his back he was filled with contempt, referring to him as 'that fat pig'.

While Hicks was running around trying to get rich his work in the property office did not go unnoticed. Senior police were watching – but they didn't quite catch on. In fact, they were so pleased with Hicks's efforts he was actually given a commendation for lowering the amount of drugs kept in the containers and therefore reducing the security risk.

It was only years later that police realised he had been selling them out the back door.

As part of his rehabilitation Hicks was moved from assistant property steward back to an investigative role in an active crew, a 'promotion' he was forced to accept even if it meant he would have to take a pay cut. 'He just went back to his old ways and did bugger all,' one colleague said.

Eventually Hicks transferred to the Benalla CIB where his boss was a Sergeant Denis Tanner.

Tanner was himself to become the subject of public controversy when he was accused of the murder of his sister-in law, Jennifer, found shot dead in 1984 in a case that was first written off as suicide.

Tanner and Hicks had both worked at the major crime squad and did not get on. But they found themselves on the same side when Hicks was later charged with corruption offences. Tanner went to a local Chief Inspector to demand to know what was happening with Hicks.

He was told it related to old matters at the drug squad. The chief inspector then said, 'It's amazing how old matters can come back to bite you on the arse.'

Tanner just looked back and said, 'Yeah, tell me about it.'

WHEN a small group of former police turned up to a subdued gathering at The Park Hotel in Abbotsford it was a little like a wake where the corpse turned up to say goodbye.

It was a Monday and Hicks knew he wouldn't be seeing his friends on the outside again for at least four years. By that Thursday he would be sitting in the dock of the Supreme Court and then would be taken directly to jail.

There would be no jury fight. He would plead guilty and ask for mercy.

It was not a night for big drinking and war stories. It was

subdued night when those old mates who turned up deliberately ignored the fact that Hicks had admitted he was a crook.

But many old associates didn't arrive. Some were angry because they had believed Hicks' repeated assurance over two years that he was innocent.

Many were stunned when Hicks pleaded guilty. His street smart barrister, Joe Gullaci, gave every indication he intended to fight the case before walking back into the Supreme Court after a lunch break to say his client would admit his guilt.

Legal sources said some thought Pilarinos was about to plead guilty and was looking for a deal. If Pilarinos had rolled over and given evidence against Hicks, the former policeman would have been looking at ten years inside.

Instead a deal was done and he was told he was likely to get four years. He decided to cut his losses.

Hicks sat in the dock in the Supreme Court on 9 March, 2000. On either side sat police. To his right was a handful of old friends from the squads. To his left were the investigators who put him there. Another former policeman, Lachlan McCulloch, went to the court to watch the man who sold him out finally admit his guilt.

Wearing a grey suit, striped tie and gold-framed spectacles, Hicks sat with his head cocked to the right as he listened to the witnesses speak on his behalf. He stood and, with a slight lisp, gave his occupation as a truck driver.

He didn't appear to be wearing a watch. He knew he didn't need one where he was going.

Gullaci told Justice Hampel how his client had lost his friends, his job and his reputation. 'Mr Hicks was one of the failures of the system and a victim of it.'

The defence suggested a non-parole sentence of four years and prosecutor, Bill Morgan-Paylor, said we 'do not view the defence submission as inappropriate.'

It ended as an anti-climax. Hicks stood, picked up an old overnight bag at his feet, managed a thin smile and a tired wink at one former colleague before going to jail.

His bald-headed guard allowed him to shake the hands of his few mates before he was led out to face the first day of the rest of his life.

But there were no old mates there to shake McCulloch's hand.

CHAPTER 5

Good Cop, Bad Cop

'I came just about last in my squad – twenty-second out of twenty-five. It was not a brilliant start.'

LACHLAN McCulloch was a young man at a fancy dress party in Carlton when he decided to be a policeman. It was a chat with an unshaven Clint Eastwood lookalike wearing a poncho and smoking a cigar that convinced him.

The Eastwood character was, in real life, a Victorian homicide squad detective. 'He said it was just fantastic,' McCulloch was to recall years later of that pivotal moment in his life. 'He drove fast cars, caught criminals and just generally had a ball.'

Back then McCulloch was hardly the type to become the average policeman. And so it proved – he was never average.

He was to be a driven detective with an enviable arrest record, an acknowledged hero who saved a little boy's life, an accomplished undercover operative who infiltrated Australia's most dangerous crime family and, finally, a classic whistle blower who would give his career to fight corruption.

McCulloch was to become a devoted policeman, but one who did not embrace the culture of the job he loved. For that reason he did what so many of his fellow detectives could not: he turned on one of his own. He didn't hide from the truth or work around a policeman he suspected of being corrupt.

He took him on head on. And, as with most collisions at terminal velocity, there would be no survivors.

BEFORE he became a policeman Lachlan McCulloch was a private school boy from a privileged background, more interested in a good time than a career. He was a pleasant enough young bloke who did not take advantage of the many opportunities offered to him at Mentone Boys Grammar.

Each year in my late teens my father bought me a plane ticket to anywhere I wanted to go. I mostly chose exotic fishing locations in Northern Australia.

I went fishing for two weeks at a fishing lodge in the Gulf of Carpentaria on my eighteenth birthday. For my nineteenth birthday I got a return ticket to London – originally for three months. At my going-away party, I overheard my father tell my uncle that I wouldn't last ten minutes over there because I couldn't look after myself.

Maybe McCulloch wanted to prove something. He worked in hotels through Europe, was a tennis coach at a private club in England, and sold cars, fishing tackle and even pine plantations before returning to Australia.

At the age of twenty-one, he wanted to be a policeman and, more than that, a star detective. But, to the casual observer, he seemed to lack the rat cunning and the streak of ruthlessness required to make a first-rate investigator.

'I made the decision and ended up getting in. I walked into the Victoria Police Academy in January, 1984. I did my five months there, I came just about last in my squad – twenty second out of twenty-five. It was not a brilliant start.'

If detectives are supposed to be distant and impersonal types

Nicole Patterson … butchered by a monster.

Her sister described Nicole as 'the most beautiful person I have known.'

By TANYA GILES,
MARK BUTTLER
and PHILIP CULLEN

A YOUNG woman dedicated to helping others was murdered in a savage knife attack in her Northcote home.

Police are investigating whether psychotherapist Nicole Amanda Patterson knew her killer.

The body of the 28-year-old crisis counsellor, who gave advice to some clients at her home, was found in a pool of blood after an attack

Gentle: Nicole Patterson

terson was killed, said she was shocked at the crime.

"I'm shaking, I'm shaking ... it's a horrible thing," Maria said.

"She was a lovely, happy girl. When she came in (to pay the rent) she would be laughing."

Search and rescue squad members and local police spent yesterday morning knocking on doors and checking drains, roofs and back yards for signs of a weapon or other evidence.

Police said a "limited

Defaced … the cutting police found at Dupas's home.

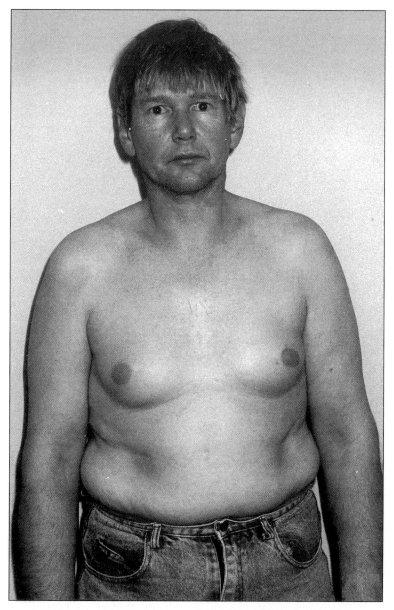

'How did you come to be as you are?'

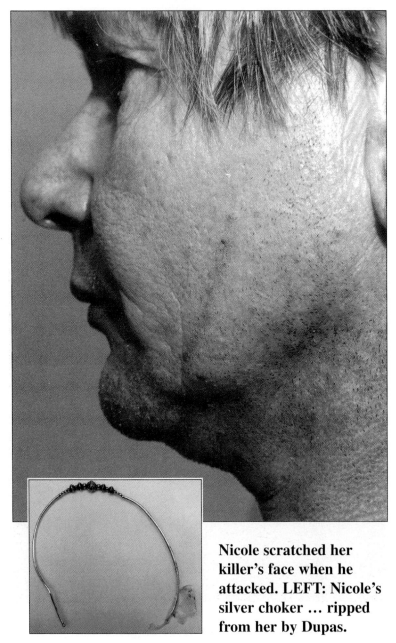

Nicole scratched her killer's face when he attacked. LEFT: Nicole's silver choker … ripped from her by Dupas.

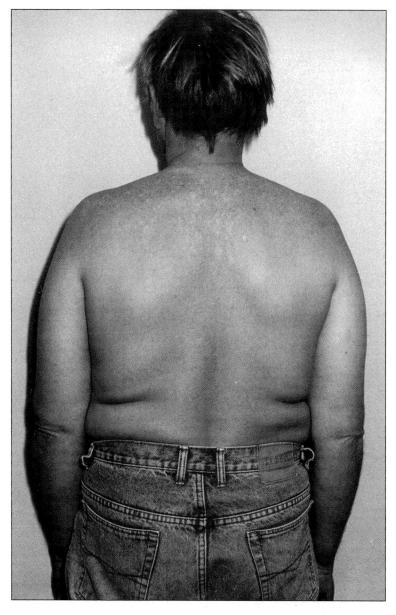

Pure evil … police photo of Dupas.

Jason Striegher: shot in the line of duty.

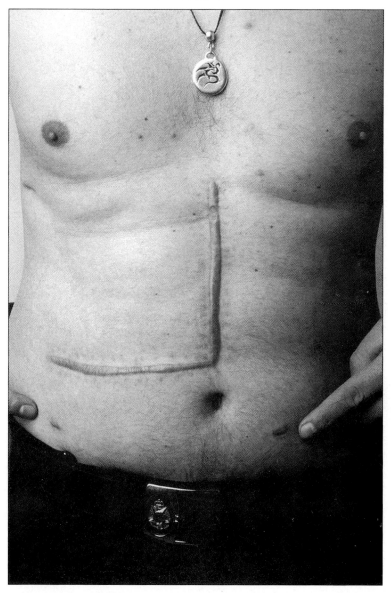

Striegher shows the entry and exit wounds and surgical
scar left by the gun battle in a suburban street.

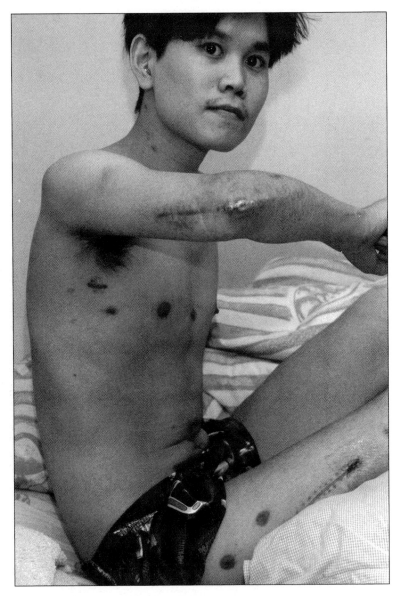

Small-time heroin dealer … big-time lucky. He survived six shots from a .357 magnum.

The end of the road for Tom Scarborough … he won't need his passport for some years.

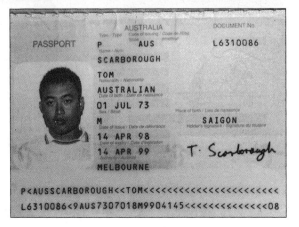

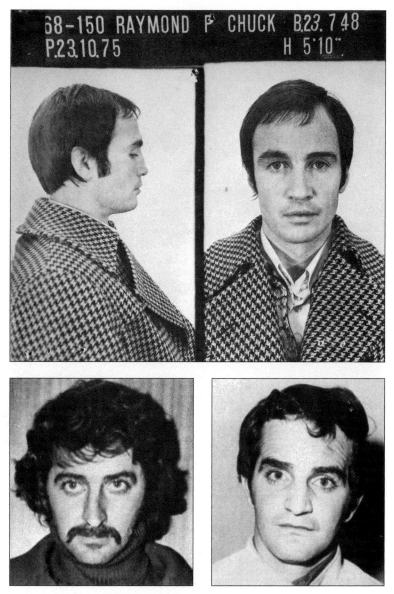

68-150 RAYMOND P CHUCK B.23.7 48
P.23.10.75 H 5'10"

**Dead men tell no tales … Raymond Chuck
(a.k.a. Bennett), Les Kane (left) and Brian Kane.**

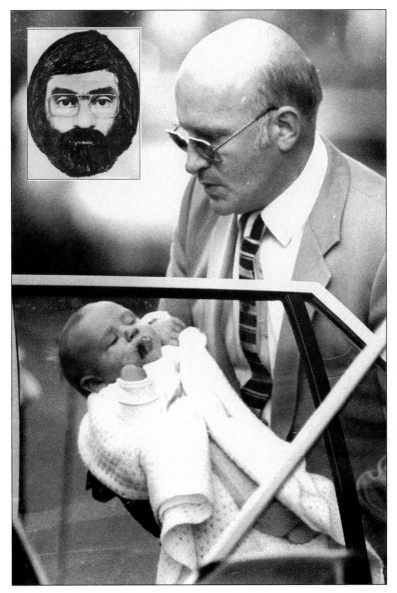

**Straight shooter Brian Murphy carries the baby.
Inset: An artist's impression of the courtroom killer.**

Tough cop turned scriptwriter. Gordon Davie rides shotgun after Ray Bennett's murder.

Under the pumpie … police looking for the courtroom killer. They didn't find him.

RIP … the gunman's ultimate occupational hazard: his own funeral.

Outside the Supreme Court two months earlier there was saturation security for Bennett. What happened?

He went that way … reporter Tony Wright and a much younger author, Andrew Rule, outside the court.

A hole in the story … the final exit in a
dream getaway for the courtroom killer.

A young terrier, Lachlan McCulloch, and the drug list he pieced together that was to expose police corruption.

who can deal with disasters and crime without emotion, then McCulloch was always going to struggle.

But, whether by design or necessity, McCulloch took his own path. Instead of trying to be something he wasn't, he used his own personality to be his type of policeman.

'As a kid I cried during every episode of *Lassie* and *Kimba the White Lion*. I get emotional about most things. I never had the makings to be a hard-boiled copper, but being a round peg that didn't fit in the police department square hole proved to be a great advantage.'

Although he was different, like most young police he quickly found the sense of power seductive.

Inside the police station a new trainee is the lowest in the food chain, but outside he wears the recognisable uniform of authority and carries the ultimate trapping of power – a loaded gun.

He had been out of the academy for just two days and was on night shift when he was told to pick up a Chinese supper for the station crew.

I picked it up and found myself in the city driving a real police car. I was all by myself. I stopped the marked police car in the middle of the road at the very top of Bourke Street. I looked down the hill towards the Mall.

I turned the blue lights and both sirens on, planted the foot and roared down Bourke Street. It was fantastic … all the large shop windows reflected the blue lights back towards me and the sound bounced off the concrete arcades … it felt good. I was a cop.

About a month later he was trusted to go out on patrol and pulled in to a 7/11 store. As he parked he saw three hotted-up Holdens and 'a dozen or so young bucks milling around.'

'*I walked in to the store and did the toughest thing I could think of. I purchased a large multi-coloured, multi-flavoured Slurpie.*'

McCulloch walked out with his Slurpie and hopped into the police car knowing he was being watched. He spun the wheels and completed a 'reverse donut' covering the onlookers in a cloud of tyre smoke.

'I only did it because I could. I didn't think I represented the law in the early days, I tended to think I was the law.'

He'd fallen into his career by a quirk of circumstance, but he soon became entranced. It was real-life drama that gave him the sense of direction that he had lacked earlier in life. He broke up with his girlfriend and spent most of his waking moments being a cop. But he was soon to learn that not every policeman shared his enthusiasm and that not all problems could be solved by the law.

I was driving past a park and there was an old, grey panel van pulled over on the side of the road with two people in it. My partner asked me to check them while he ran the registration through D24.

I looked in the driver's door window. There was a young bloke, about twenty – he was leaning over and in the passenger seat was a young girl of about fifteen. She was leaning back in the seat looking at the ceiling, The guy in the driver's seat was injecting a syringe into her eye.

I couldn't believe it and just froze. I couldn't grab him because he had the needle in her eye and I was scared that I would cause her more damage. I was torn between grabbing him and not grabbing him. Anyway, it felt like ages, but it was probably only a few seconds before he finished.

I reached in and grabbed the hand holding the syringe, knocking the syringe onto the floor. I put my left arm around his throat, my elbow under his chin and dragged him backwards out the driver's window onto the road. I then knelt on the back of his head pushing his face into the roadway, and handcuffed him. I dragged him over to the grass by his hair; I couldn't hear him screaming. By this time my partner jumped out to see what's going on.

As for the girl in the passenger seat, the heroin had basically gone straight into her brain and she was unconscious. We carried her limp body onto the grassy verge next to the park. Next thing I remember two girls pulled up in a passing car and jumping out asked if they could help. I said, 'No, no, please get in your car and leave'. They explained to me that they were nurses and could actually help, so I asked them to check the girl as she'd overdosed or something.

A few minutes later the ambulance arrived and injected her with Narcan, which instantly reverses the effects of the heroin. I wanted to kill the man who had done this to her.

I dragged him over to the back of the divisional van, my partner grabbed me by the arm and said, 'Hang on a second.' I let him go. I put him on the ground again and walked back to the car to talk to my partner.

He said, 'Listen, have a look.' He held up his watch and said: 'Come on, we've got ten minutes till we knock off, it's Sunday.' He directed me to uncuff the guy and let him go. I uncuffed him, walked back to the car and sat there in total disbelief. Letting him go was against everything I ever dreamed and believed in.

I was there to fight crime, not finish work on time. I truly believed. I believed I could make a difference. Letting him go was condoning everything I was against. To a young cop like me – it was devastating.

The inexperienced police constable was sent to work at one of the busiest stations in Melbourne – Richmond – and got a crash course in street policing.

As a keen angler, he knew the value of finding a productive fishing hole to which he could return again and again for a bag. As a policeman he soon learned that the same principal worked in the underworld. If he stayed close to the house of a notorious drug dealer called Dennis 'Mr Death' Allen (who died in 1987) he would catch as many criminals as he could handle.

'Every shift you just drove around looking for taxis and things in the area, just pulling over anybody that looked suspicious. Nearly every time they either had $90 to buy heroin or they had heroin in their possession they had just bought. They'd also take heaps of stolen goods and jewellery to various places. They'd be in stolen cars at times; the area was full of crooks.

'You just caught crook after crook and the only thing that held you back was the time it took to process them, either lock them up and remand them or, if they gave you information, they somehow got bail.'

When McCulloch left the academy he was seen as a plodder, but he adapted quickly on the street. He was the first in his squad to make detective.

He worked at Richmond, Reservoir and the City traffic branch, but he had his eye on a position in the toughest, and sometimes dirtiest, stations in the state: St Kilda.

One of Victoria's most experienced policeman was working at the station and remembered McCulloch when he first arrived. 'He was as green as grass and keen as mustard. He never stopped.' Another recalled: 'He always reminded me of a little Jack Russell. He would clamp on to something and wouldn't let go.'

McCulloch worked in uniform for about twelve months before he moved into plain clothes, let his hair grow and began to hone his natural skills as an undercover operative.

He was eventually to develop his own street character – an unwashed street vagrant known as 'Dean Collie'.

'I really tried to look like the loser from hell – a drop kick. I thought I looked like a dog, a collie, so Dean Collie was born.'

He bought a long brown wig and streaked it with animal fat to look like unwashed hair, wedged strips of toilet paper under his lips to give the puffy look of an alcoholic, wore an old fishing jacket, oversized pants and worn-out snow boots.

He learned to rub his eyes to redden them so that he looked like a drug user and developed the habitual sniff of an addict. He could walk the streets observing activities that would escape most police – in uniform or plain clothes. He would then return 'on-duty' to use that information to make arrests. He found work to be fun but was reminded time and again that it was life and death and no act. He could only watch as a young female addict he knew slowly killed herself with heroin. The most he could do for her was to adopt her three-legged cat, Indi.

He was present when a fellow policeman shot and killed a Canberra jail escapee, Arthur Nelson, in St Kilda on 27 July, 1988.

He received a Chief Commissioner's Commendation for bravery when he saved a child from a dangerous man in September, 1990.

He was commended for initiative and diligence and again praised when he ran an operation in Carlton that resulted in the arrest of thirty-five offenders on 184 charges, including attempted murder.

McCulloch, the former under-achieving schoolboy, was on his way to being a star. He policed with a passion and got results.

In 1991 he transferred to the drug squad and became an undercover operative with the code number 004.

'I spent the whole time trying not to act like a cop, and not to think like one. This meant that my whole demeanour was not one of a typical cop. This meant that to many cops, I didn't fit in.'

IF THERE was one crime family in Australia considered beyond infiltration by undercover police it was the Pettingills. The mother, Kath, had been around crime for thirty years and knew most of the tricks. Two of her sons, Victor Peirce and Trevor Pettingill, had been charged and acquitted of the 1988 Walsh Street murders of Constables Damian Eyre and Steven Tynan.

To investigate the Pettingills was seen as dangerous on two fronts. They were blamed for Walsh Street and were seen as capable of killing and they were likely to claim harassment if they were targeted without water-tight evidence.

But McCulloch had an informer connected with the family and was keen to try. Senior police were concerned about the risks, but eventually gave their boyish-looking undercover the nod to set up some meetings. McCulloch didn't try to out-macho the crooks. He became Lenny Rogers, a shy former public school boy who wanted to sell drugs to yuppies on the ski slopes. His investigations resulted in two taskforces, Earthquake and Tremor. Fifteen people, including Kath and Trevor, were arrested and marijuana, heroin and amphetamines rings were smashed.

Again he was highly commended for 'dedication to duty, covert skills and exceptional courage.'

Policing was turning out to be as good as the detective he met at the fancy dress party had described. It was fun and you could make a difference. But there was to be a downside.

IT WAS 1.22pm on 8 April, 1992, when McCulloch received a message to ring the Selby Medical and Scientific Supplies. A man named James Sweetin had made some questionable purchases that needed checking.

The next day he went to the company's Mulgrave office and was given a list of chemicals and lab gear the man had bought. Sweetin was clearly setting up to produce speed.

Quickly McCulloch gathered evidence and was able to trace Sweetin to Peter Pilarinos, a gangster figure well known to police. His brother owned a St Kilda nightclub often used for detective functions and fund raisers.

McCulloch went to Pilarinos's huge home, spread over three big blocks on a hill in Doncaster. On 13 June at 4.35am he ratted through his suspect's wheelie bin and found two recipes for speed that had been ripped up and stuffed in tin of dog food.

Next to the chemical 'methylamine' was written '$0.00'. What McCulloch didn't know was this was because it had already been stolen from the drug squad compound in Attwood in a scheme authorised by a corrupt police officer.

But while he did not yet know about the drug break-in he was soon to learn he was being sold out. Sweetin's phone was being tapped and on 29 September police monitored a phone call from Sweetin to drug associate, Ken Milton, who said he was about to find out if the phone was bugged. When he rang back he was in no doubt. 'Don't say my name, treat your rear vision mirrors like guardian angels, treat this thing like everybody is listening.'

The next day police broke into a house in Ferntree Gully which was being used as the speed lab. All the equipment had been re-boxed. The gang had been tipped off and had cancelled their 'cook'.

McCulloch was disappointed but not heart broken. There were more crims to catch and he wasn't going to dwell on the one that got away. But what sometimes kept him awake at night was that he was sold out and that Pilarinos and his gang had at least one detective on his payroll.

McCulloch had two Polaroid photographs taken from a surveillance video and stuck one of Sweetin on his grey locker to the left of his desk. During Operation Cane it mysteriously went missing.

A few months earlier Kevin Hicks had arrived at the squad after being sacked from the major crime squad for laziness. The majors were in terminal decline and were about to be disbanded.

Hicks was now the assistant property steward in charge of drug exhibits. It was a catastrophic fall down the pecking order, but Hicks still had a wealth of experience and McCulloch liked to talk to the older detective. Hicks would stop and chat to the operational detectives, asking them what was going on. Most thought he was just missing the action. What he was really doing was selling them out for envelopes of cash ranging from $500 to $2500.

McCulloch asked Hicks if he knew Pilarinos. The former major crime squad detective looked him in the eye and said no.

He examined surveillance photos of the Doncaster house and showed a great deal of interest in a case he was not involved in.

Some detectives see rats in the rank as an occupational hazard.

They try to work around suspect police without confronting their suspicions. For a man like McCulloch, who wore his heart on his sleeve, the idea of being sold out was shattering.

In 1993 McCulloch learnt that Hicks had known Pilarinos for years and was lying. It was then he started to think the detective's interest in his case may have been more than passing.

'I trusted Hicks. He went out of his way to ask me about my Operation (Cane). I told him everything. I considered him a friend. I also wanted to impress him with my investigations. He betrayed my trust. In my investigative detective world selling out my job to the main target, Peter Pilarinos, was about the worst thing one detective could do to another.'

The open and talkative McCulloch started to chip away at Pilarinos, but keep some of the information to himself. It was to be three years before it began to come together.

IN APRIL 1995 McCulloch was upgraded to acting detective sergeant and was able to start his own investigations. He immediately targeted Pilarinos in Operation Austin.

By May he had enough information to have a tap put on the home phone of his target. A man named Steve started to ring regularly. He was a man who was clearly close to the target, but his identity was a mystery.

McCulloch was driven but not obsessed with the case, and when he came to work early one Thursday morning his thumping hangover meant that Panadol rather the Pilarinos was the first thing on his mind. He had been to a huge drug squad party the previous night. It was to be the last turn at the old Police Club in Mackenzie Street and for Lachlan it had been a big one. He reported to the Special Projects Unit at St Kilda Road to monitor Pilarinos's phone. He was glad that duty that day would be quiet rather than involving arrests and raids.

On the phone he could hear Steve talking. He, too, was hung-over and he was telling Pilarinos what a big night it had been. 'It slowly dawned on me that 'Steve' had been to the same party and was probably a copper.'

McCulloch identified a pager number that belonged to Steve and rang it. The polite woman at the paging service said she could not pass on the name of the client as he was a detective sergeant of police. Years later, that man was still in the force.

McCulloch listened to many calls where Steve and Pilarinos discussed the man they called 'K' or 'Fat Boy from up north.' It was Hicks, who had moved from the drug squad and was stationed at Benalla. Within two days of McCulloch identifying 'Steve' and Hicks as dealing with Pilarinos his drug squad office was burgled.

If he needed any confirmation that he was being sold out it came when he heard Pilarinos planning a drug drop off in St Kilda in one hour. This was the break he wanted and McCulloch raced to Wellington Street for the triumphant arrest. As McCulloch moved in to make the grab his man Pilarinos turned, smiled and said, 'So you're Lachlan.'

There were no drugs. 'He just wanted to see who was after him.'

What began as an interesting and challenging drug investigation was turning into a murky corruption investigation. Many police weren't quite sure where it would lead and just as many didn't want to find out.

If McCulloch was going to fight he knew he would be opposed to corrupt police who would do anything to destroy him and a culture where few would stand up for him. The police culture is often referred to as 'The Brotherhood' and for good reasons. Families protect their own – even the black sheep. Police will only turn on their own when the evidence is overwhelming. Loyalty makes them believe the lamest alibi if it means they don't have to confront the fact that a colleague is bent.

Many police now condemn Hicks as a traitor, but few were

prepared to side with McCulloch when he first blew the whistle. The young detective who joined the job to catch crooks was being sucked into a world where he would become an internal investigator, a 'toe-cutter', and he would be unpopular because of it.

Confused loyalties made him, to some, the enemy. Some saw him as obsessed and wondered why he was running a campaign against a harmless country copper and his drug dealing mate.

But, after more than ten years in the job, McCulloch knew the consequences of what he was doing.

Like the New York policeman, Frank Serpico, he was prepared to sacrifice his career to fight corruption and, like Serpico, he was made an outsider from 'The Brotherhood.'

The day I chose to begin this was the day I knew I would eventually have to leave the job. I decided that night I had no future in the police force and that I would declare war on whoever was behind this.

I went up to a pub in Carlton with a group of detectives and told them where I was. I wanted them to join in and take them on. One said he wasn't prepared to be involved. He said he might end up getting glassed at a police turn. Other members said they didn't want to play because the stakes were so high.

I got home from work, and feebly attempted to tell my wife what had happened. Of course this was useless as she is not in 'The Job', and cannot comprehend what I was going through, so I opened a cask of chablis and proceeded to communicate with it.

I found myself sitting in the loungeroom looking out the window, thinking I don't deserve this. I just want to catch a crook. But I'm now up to my arse in corruption. Who do I trust?

Full of bad wine and melancholy he grabbed his diving gear and went to the beach, swum out and sunk to the bottom in five metres of water. It was nearly midnight. He lay on the bottom at peace until he ran out of air. When he was forced to surface he found himself yelling 'Bastards' in the general direction of the West Gate Bridge. There was no-one who could hear him.

He knew his decision to fight Pilarinos would come at a price.

'It was detrimental to my future, personally and professionally. For some reason I took police corruption personally. I thought it was up to me to make a difference. I had seen so many people look away, walk away. I knew how damaging Hicks was. Every honest drug squad cop would be tarred by his actions.'

Police launched an internal inquiry into Hicks and 'Steve', the detective sergeant caught talking to Pilarinos, but failed to gather sufficient evidence to justify charges.

McCulloch developed his own strategy. He would pound Pilarinos and his colleagues until they cracked. He harassed them and used every trick he could think of. It there were rules he threw them out. He investigated anyone connected with his major target. It had become intensely personal.

Pilarinos hated McCulloch. He was heard to threaten the detective's life. In one phone tap from jail he was recorded suggesting sodomy wasn't out of the question. He also wanted to know why this zealot couldn't be 'got at'.

'Pilarinos was very affable and charming, the sort who would use you up then drop you like a hot cake. But he hated Lachlan like you wouldn't believe,' one detective recalled.

But the young detective was now a man on a mission. In 1996 he formed another investigative team, code named Redalen, and in August arrested James Sweetin at an amphetamines lab in Bayswater.

Sweetin finally admitted it was Hicks who was the corrupt policeman supplying information and drugs to Pilarinos. He said that Hicks had supplied the keys to the drug squad lock-up and they had burgled the containers to steal back chemicals seized in earlier raids.

If McCulloch thought the admission was a breakthrough he

didn't know how hard it was to catch a bent cop. An ethical standards department taskforce, code named Guardsman, was formed. Lachlan was seconded to work for it and was branded as a toe-cutter and a traitor to the drug squad.

'He was vilified by some who should hang their heads in shame now. People still backed Hicks. McCulloch was called a dog and a maggot. But he wasn't the one who sold them out,' an investigator from Guardsman said.

McCulloch started to carry a gun twenty four hours a day and had a sophisticated security system installed to protect his home.

But there is a more effective way to destroy a detective than using violence. A murdered copper is a martyr – a compromised one is toothless.

McCULLOCH could not be a dispassionate internal investigator. He had been fighting this battle for years and it could never be just another case for him. But Pilarinos was fighting for his freedom and a rat is most dangerous when cornered.

Out of nowhere rumours started to spread that McCulloch was corrupt, that he had been selling out jobs, trafficked heroin, sold guns to crooks and organised two murders. He had a nice house in a bayside suburb and it wasn't long before some started to ask how he could afford it

He was at home cooking some sausages at a family barbecue one night when a *Four Corners* reporter walked in and began to ask questions about police corruption. From the tone of the conversation McCulloch could tell he was not considered a whistle blower but a crook. It is believed Peter Pilarinos was the source of the information.

Even though no-one believed the rumours senior officers did not want Guardsman compromised, so they decided to move McCulloch. He was considered expendable.

He could not go back to the drug squad so he was sent to a

suburban CIB. Within days he was confronted by an older detective who said he was a friend of the Pilarinos family and there was no place for McCulloch in that office. Later, an inspector made it clear he should move on. A senior policeman chastised the inspector, but he kept his position while McCulloch was transferred.

He was moved to the rape squad. 'They put me in a place where there was no corruption. We just investigated serial sickos.'

Some senior police didn't have the stomach for a long and messy investigation into Hicks with no guarantees of success. One suggested they should gather just enough evidence to charge him with discipline and not criminal charges. He could then be just quietly sacked. Another suggested that police should just follow Steve, the detective sergeant suspected of being crooked, when he went the pub so they could breathalyze him on the way home. While it wasn't exactly sweeping corruption under the carpet it would stop any damning headlines about bent coppers while quietly getting rid of them.

But the investigators resisted and on 19 May, 1997, Pilarinos and Hicks were arrested. Hicks knew it was coming. He said nothing to the investigators, but he said plenty to others.

He told any policeman who would listen that he was innocent. It was a frame up and he would fight it.

One detective who is probably lucky he didn't end up in the dock with Hicks said the case was a 'souffle' – a hard crust with nothing but hot air in the middle.

So it came as a surprise when Hick pleaded guilty. He thought Pilarinos would roll over and give evidence against him and if that happened he would do ten years. Now he was told a deal could be done and he could look at six years with a minimum of four.

Pilarinos was outraged. He, too, pleaded guilty but his bargaining chips had already been cashed. He made a statement on police corruption to investigators, but there were more allegations than substance. He may have known where the bodies were buried but he wouldn't help dig deep. He told enough to try to save himself, but it wasn't enough.

Pilarinos had been the associate of police and criminals for many years and would have been able to stay out of jail by providing information.

In certain underworld circles it had been alleged he had been more than helpful to police who were hunting 'Mad Max' – Pavel Marinoff, the Bulgarian Army deserter who shot six Victorian police in 1985-86.

Several violent criminals in jail said they would welcome the chance to 'catch-up' with the former mate of many detectives. His actions over the years had turned him from a protected species to an endangered one. But McCulloch was also a casualty. He could not go back to being an 'ordinary' detective. He knew he was drinking too much and brooding. The fun had gone out of policing. He no longer felt he belonged, but he stayed loyal: 'I loved my time in the drug squad and I don't want people thinking there are crooks there. Hicks was a problem and he is now in jail. The good guys have won and the squad can get on with catching drug dealers.'

In his resignation letter from November 1999 he wrote: 'I have had an absolute ball over the last 16 years. I am proud to have been a member of the Victoria Police Force.'

The irony is that if Hicks could have controlled his greed and not sold out McCulloch in Operation Cane they would both still be in the force. One is no loss. The other is a tragic one.

IN late May, 2000, Lachlan McCulloch sat in the Supreme Court public gallery above court three and heard the cultured voice of Justice George Hampel as he sentenced the two men in the dock. One was Kevin Hicks – the other, Peter Pilarinos. Both were going to jail and McCulloch knew he was responsible for sending them there.

Even though it was his moment McCulloch felt no sense of triumph – just a wave of relief that his eight-year battle to expose police corruption was finally over.

Many former police colleagues who had branded him as obsessed over his fight to find out who had sold out his investigations into Pilarinos, were now silent.

McCulloch had often felt alone and wondered who he could trust. Now, nearly seven months after he quit the force, he was vindicated at last. He had been right all along – no-one would be able to doubt what he had done.

In the Supreme Court McCulloch drew comfort from those around him. He was flanked by drug detectives, including the head of the squad, Detective Chief Inspector John McKoy.

About a month earlier McKoy rang his former detective. He said that if McCulloch intended to go to the sentencing, 'I would be proud to walk into court with you.'

The public act of solidarity was not lost on McCulloch. He knew he had the support of the vast majority of police in Victoria. The snipers who had turned on him had been discredited. A policewoman he didn't know wrote to him to say she was ashamed of the way he had been treated. Others contacted him to congratulate him.

A woman wrote to *The Age:* 'Take a bow Lachlan McCulloch. What courage you have, your integrity is impeccable. Your family must be proud of you. You are a wonderful role model.' But the senior policeman who kicked him off the Guardsman taskforce and the inspector who didn't want him at his suburban CIB were not among those who wanted to pat McCulloch on the back.

'It has been a difficult time for me and I appreciate the support I have had from Mr McKoy, other members of the drug squad and the ethical standards department. Mr McKoy always encouraged me to investigate the corruption,' he said.

As the drug squad chief and his whistle blower sat in the gallery, the corrupt detective and his partner sat in the dock below – neither acknowledging the presence of the other.

The discredited policeman, and the career crook would not look at each other. They could have been strangers waiting for a bus, not the core of a corrupt group responsible for stealing drugs from a police storage depot and reselling them.

They would have got away with it, if it hadn't been for McCulloch and his campaign to find out who was the rat in the drug squad ranks. It allowed Ethical Standards Department investigators such as Wayne Taylor, Adrian White and Keith McManamny to build the case that resulted in the arrest of Hicks and Pilarinos in 1997.

Hicks pleaded guilty. Yes, he had sold out police operations and yes, he had helped Pilarinos sell drugs. Now he sat in the dock, wearing his grey suit, steel rimmed spectacles, and Blundstone boots. He had been led to believe that he was likely to get six years with a minimum of four years jail and seemed resigned to it.

George Hampel is not considered the toughest sentencer in the Supreme Court. Some police complain he can be too compassionate and lenient for their tastes.

But Justice Hampel is his own man. The defence and prosecution thought they had a deal. but they forgot that the judge calls the shots. Hicks was sentenced to seven and a half years with a non-parole period of five years.

As Hicks heard the sentence details and realised he was getting more jail time than he expected he let out a little sigh and blinked slowly. It reminded onlookers of his old nick-name – 'Koala Bear'.

Pilarinos came next. Justice Hampel said claims that he was an important witness in ongoing police corruption matters had been 'overstated'. He made the point that while the defence had told him Pilarinos was feeling 'genuine remorse' for his life of crime and was prepared to expose corruption, the defendant had chosen to remain silent on his own involvement in the drug squad thefts.

Justice Hampel said the person who offered the bribe and the one who accepted were equally culpable.

He sentenced Pilarinos to eight and a half years with a minimum of six.

Chief Commissioner, Neil Comrie, said later: 'This result sends a clear message that the Force can police itself and weed out unprofessional and unethical officers.

'The force will do everything possible to ensure any corrupt officers are removed from the ranks of the Victoria Police. The public would expect nothing less.'

As the two guilty men were led out of court Pilarinos's youngest son ran to embrace him. The young man's grief turned quickly to anger as he swore at a court guard and punched the door on his way out.

Outside the court, McCulloch walked down the stairs. The son turned his anger on the whistle blower. 'You are nothing but a f...... dog. I hope you rot in Hell.'

McCulloch did not respond – he didn't need to. He had won. Mrs Valerie Pilarinos, not long released from jail after completing a sentence for perjury venomously referred to McCulloch as 'Australia's Serpico' and wishing him an unpleasant after-life.

The son stood about three metres from the man who blew the whistle on his father. He glared with a hatred born from years of watching his father slowly reduced from an untouchable to just another crim going to jail in the back of a van.

McKoy and others from the drug squad were close by. They weren't going to allow McCulloch to be put in any physical danger.

Later, investigators from Operation Guardsman, who had built the case that exposed the corruption, took him for a coffee away from the biting cold and the bitter Pilarinos family. But many of the police who had loudly supported Hicks after he was charged with corruption were not in court to hear the final sentence.

The message was clear for McCulloch.

After fighting corruption for eight years and sacrificing his career of sixteen, the battle had been worthwhile.

He was not alone after all.

POSTSCRIPT: The day after the sentencing Neil Comrie rang McCulloch and asked him to lunch to thank him in private. Within a week, a senior policeman rang to ask the former detective to rejoin the force. McCulloch refused but said he would love to lecture new recruits on the ethics of policing.

He had also decided to try his hand at writing a book. The result turned out to be a blockbuster – *The Street*.

CHAPTER 6

Falling Down

*'Within seconds of me tossing the parcel I heard
a huge bang, which was similar to a huge
firecracker being let off in a small space.'*

NOBODY who knew Colin Dunstan was surprised that he finally flipped out. It was the way he did it that shocked people.

In America, they call it 'going postal' – blackly humorous shorthand for the murderous madness that can make someone take out a gun at work and start shooting until the ammunition runs out and the SWAT team runs in. The 'postal' tag comes from the fact, which has entered urban folklore, that several US mail workers have done such a thing, wreaking revenge for real or imagined grievances of the sort that fester in the souls of little people toiling for giant organisations.

Variations on a theme of being mad as hell and not taking it any more are not new, of course. They have infiltrated popular culture, feeding the revenge fantasies of loopy loners who see themselves as some sort of persecuted suburban heroes – like the out-of-control everyman that Michael Douglas plays in the film *Falling Down*, which has become a reference point for describing outbursts of extraordinary violence by otherwise ordinary men.

But Canberra is not California and, thankfully, Colin Dunstan wasn't marching to a beat that demanded an AK-47 assault rifle. When the prim and proper public servant 'went postal', he did it literally ... he made letter bombs. Not that Dunstan would agree with the 'bomb' word. At his trial, he maintained that while the twenty-eight 'devices' he posted might have resembled realistic letter bombs, they wouldn't actually explode. And, even if they did, they wouldn't hurt anyone. Much, anyway.

The problem with running that defence is that one of the devices had detonated when being handled even before it was opened. And if that hadn't happened in time to warn the authorities, then twenty-six other identical packages would have ended up in the letter boxes of people high on Dunstan's long list of 'enemies'. Any one of them, according to the police and the prosecution, had the potential to injure. And all were calculated to terrify.

It's all a long way from trouble around the tea trolley in the Australian Tax Office. But that's where Colin Dunstan's fall began.

COLIN George Dunstan's origins are as prosaic and stolid as his name suggests. The middle child – but only son – of five children born to a respectable Wollongong couple in the 1950s, he was by all accounts a conscientious boy who helped his father with his vegetable garden and hobby of breeding birds and small animals.

Young Colin worked hard at school, apparently as a way of gaining his father's praise, which he craved but felt he didn't get, a psychiatrist would later say. The diligent boy grew into a self-absorbed young man who shone in maths and science subjects, finishing in the top fifty science students in New South Wales in his final year.

He left home at eighteen years old to go to the Australian National University in Canberra, where in 1974 he met the woman who was to become his first wife. They married in 1977, the year he took his arts degree, and later had three daughters.

FALLING DOWN

Intelligent and meticulous, Dunstan had 'obsessional traits' that became more pronounced with age – and which, his psychiatrist noted drily in a report tendered in court, were shared by 'most good public servants'.

He later took woodwork, cooking and electronics classes in his own time. A lean man who kept fit and dressed neatly, he was good with his hands as well as his mind, and was attracted early to information technology. He came to be seen as something of a computer expert before a wave of younger, computer-literate staff entered the public service in the 1990s, by which time his star was rapidly dimming.

Dunstan's troubles began when he transferred to the Tax Office from another department in 1987. At age thirty-two, his psychiatrist was to testify later, he wanted a 'fresh challenge'. That is, a fresh challenge by public servant standards.

He didn't want to become a skydiving instructor or trek through the Andes. He didn't even want to do anything that would alter his daily routine of going to work in Canberra's rabbit warren of anonymous offices. All he wanted was to be appointed a Data Base Administrator.

He got the job, but trouble came with the territory. A married woman he had known slightly in 1982 in another department was one of his subordinates. She began, he was to complain later, to plague him for advice about problems. She contrived excuses to see him in person, and made it clear she was infatuated with him.

It was the beginning of a bizarre interlude in which the woman – whose name has been suppressed by court order – allegedly began to stalk Dunstan and his family. Dunstan's wife received mysterious 'hang-up' telephone calls and the woman once confronted her. When Dunstan's psychiatrist later described this period in a report, he put it under the heading *Fatal Attraction*.

Dunstan became depressed and rattled; it showed in his work and his behavior. He fell into a shortlived affair with the woman, who had pursued him for four years. This aggravated his problems and was eventually to end his marriage and his career. He became isolated from friends, family and workmates.

In early 1992, he moved out of his family home and into a flat and attempted suicide with an overdose of prescription painkillers. His worried wife, meanwhile, approached the other woman's husband to try to end what she saw as years of harassment.

The already bizarre situation spun out of control and began to involve others when the woman complained to an equal opportunity officer, who allegedly took her side and wrote a letter suggesting that the Dunstans had 'intimidated and harassed' the woman.

Dunstan's version of events, as told to his psychiatrist and lawyers, is that the woman orchestrated a revenge campaign against him by making spurious complaints to his superiors and to the Human Rights and Equal Opportunities Commission.

The Tax Office responded by trying to make it go away – transferring both Duncan and the woman to other sections.

Dunstan recovered from his suicide attempt and continued his struggle against the system with renewed bitterness. By then divorced from his wife, he met and married another woman in 1994 who encouraged his belief that he was a victim. It seemed to him that while the other woman continued to be promoted, his own career had been stalled, if not derailed. In his mind, he'd been made a scapegoat for a mess not of his making, while the real culprit was going unpunished.

And he believed that other people now involved in the dispute had unfairly sided against him, pre-judging his case so that the more he tried to prove his point, the more they opposed him. All of which might have sounded like just another paranoid delusion, but the factual basis of Dunstan's dilemma was not lost on the judge who sifted through the facts. Though nothing excused Dunstan's actions, the judge was to say, it was clear why he had such a grievance against the system. But that was later.

FALLING DOWN

FOR Nelly Campbell, it was just another nightshift at the Canberra mail centre in Fyshwick, the faintly industrial underbelly of the model modern city.

On December 1, 1998, a Tuesday evening, the thirty-five year-old mother started at 6pm sharp, as she usually did, intending to work until exactly 1.51am next morning.

Nelly Campbell and three workmates started the shift by moving a big steel crate of unsorted parcels into what they call the 'bull ring', then sorting them into a series of tubs. At 7.45pm, they switched to 'indexing' – typing postcodes on envelopes so that they could be easily and accurately sorted. At 9.25pm, the crew had a rest break, starting again at 10pm on a new task. At midnight, they started the last job of the night – sorting small parcels. The crew sorted the first crate of parcels in about fifteen minutes, then Campbell fetched another bin and they started work.

'We had only been sorting this particular bin for about a minute or two,' she was to recall, 'when I picked up two small white-colored parcels. I checked the suburb and postcode and tossed the (first) parcel in the Queanbeyan area bin. As soon as I had done this I realised I had mis-sorted the parcel – meaning I had tossed it into the wrong bin. While I still had one of the parcels in my hand I picked up another parcel which looked exactly the same as the one I had tossed and the same as the one I still had in my hand.

'I checked the suburb and postcode and this time leaned so I was closer to the tub and wouldn't mis-sort and tossed the parcel into the tub. Within seconds I heard a huge bang, which was similar to a huge firecracker being let off in a small space. At first, I saw a white light coming from the tub and then I saw smoke. (It) filled the area where I was standing. I could smell what I thought was gunpowder ... I felt things hitting me but I didn't realise what they were.

'I looked down and saw a lot of blue plastic pieces. That's when I realised what had hit me.' Two senior mail officers grabbed the tub and moved it away from the workers.

Nelly Campbell's ears were ringing, one arm felt numb and she was gripped by the shock that was to stop her working for eight months. But she remembered she'd seen more than a dozen parcels identical to the one that had exploded, and said so. They were all about the size of a computer disc, she said, but about two centimetres thick, and wrapped in white paper, with addresses neatly printed. Each had two stamps – a two dollar blackwood tree stamp and a thirty-cent saltwater crocodile stamp.

All neat and tidy, like scones from the same perfect batch.

ACTING Sergeant Mark Johnsen, of the Federal Police, took the call about 3am. By the time he got to the mail centre, the bomb experts and forensic police had secured the scene and started the painstaking job of gathering evidence. Which, in this case, meant more than just using vacuum equipment and tapelifts to gather explosive propellant residue and broken plastic.

They had to look for letter bombs and disable them. The police worked all night. By seven o'clock that morning, they had twenty-one identical white parcels and were satisfied there were no more in the mail exchange. But the police knew what the public didn't: that a letter bomb had been detected and defused in Sydney the day before, and that it matched the twenty they now had.

So how many more were there in the postal system? There was no way of knowing how many had been sent, or where, until the offender was found.

The police hit the telephones. The first lead: the return address on each of the suspect parcels had the name 'D. O'DONNELL' and a Canberra street and suburb. Then there were the names and addresses on each of the twenty-one parcels.

It didn't take long to establish that one Daniel O'Donnell had nothing to do with sending the letter bombs – but there was a connection. His mother was a public servant who'd had dealings with someone known to twenty-one other potential recipients.

FALLING DOWN

By mid-morning, a flurry of telephone calls, followed with flying visits, had established that they were all linked by one thing. When each was asked if he or she knew anyone who might make and send letter bombs, most nominated Colin Dunstan.

The police converged on Dunstan's house in Palmerston in early afternoon. First, trained negotiators had telephoned the house to ensure that Dunstan was not holding his wife hostage. He wasn't. Knowing police were on the way, Dunstan's wife, Sokkha Hac, took some computer disks and threw them over her back fence, a court was later told.

The police recovered the disks, but there was no retrievable information left on them. There was, however, other evidence in and around the house that matched grains of gunpowder, pieces of plastic and other material they'd found at the mail exchange.

Now they were sure of their man, but not where he was. One thing was sure: if his wife knew, she wasn't saying.

POLICE in every state were watching for the Canberra letter bomber. His photograph and description had been circulated nation-wide; every airport was alerted in case he tried to flee the country. But the wanted man was closer to home than anyone imagined.

On the Tuesday morning, more than twelve hours before the furore at the mail centre, a man driving a undistinguished blue Toyota Corona drove into the Curtin Budget Motel, a small motel near a riding school about ten minutes from the city.

He booked in, giving his name to the duty manager as Ron White, and was shown to room six. The motel owner, Les McCabe, was interested to see the name in the ledger because he had worked with a Ron White in Sydney years before, and wondered if it was the same man. McCabe was left wondering that day because the man stayed in his room.

A long-term resident in the next room noticed an odd thing

about the quiet man in number six. Each morning that week, 'Ron White' got up when his alarm went at 6am, started his Toyota precisely fifteen minutes later and let it idle for quarter of an hour before driving off in the direction of the nearest McDonald's store. In an era when few people bother warming car motors, it seemed an elaborately painstaking routine.

The guest had paid $150 in advance for three nights. On Friday, his last morning, he went to reception and offered $20 to be able to check out late, at noon. The McCabes noticed he still hadn't left when they began their lunch, but they weren't overly concerned. When Les McCabe returned to the office the guest was waiting for him. He was sitting outside the door trying to hide the fact he was holding a bloodsoaked wad of paper to one wrist.

McCabe grabbed the paper and had a look. There were two deep cuts in the man's arm. He had obviously lost a lot of blood. McCabe bundled him into the car and drove him to hospital.

Left to cool his heels in the casualty waiting room, McCabe started to sense something odd when he inquired about 'Ron White' with a nurse, and no patient of that name came up on the computer screen. McCabe also noticed that the nurse looked unusually flustered. What he didn't know until later was that she had just called the police because the suicidal patient virtually admitted he was the letter bomber, and had asked for his lawyer to be called. He also said he had taken a drug overdose and would die of liver failure within days.

Still unaware of the drama unfolding around him, McCabe left the mysterious guest to it and drove back to the motel – only to find it surrounded by police cars and news crews. The police blocked his way, and when he identified himself they put him in a car with two detectives who questioned him.

It was then he found out that the guest in room six was Australia's most wanted man. It turned out that while he was at the hospital his wife had gone to clean the room. She found blood in the bathroom and a note on a table saying there were no weapons or bombs in the room and requesting the finder to tell his wife that he'd put money in the bank to pay the mortgage.

Mrs McCabe knew the guest had to be the letter bomber. She called the police, only to be told that she was probably mistaken because they believed Dunstan had fled to Queensland.

Half an hour later, a constable turned up and acknowledged that the blue Toyota looked like Dunstan's car, but had the wrong number plates. But when he found the car's correct plates in a bag in the front seat there was no doubt about it. He had a quick look at room six and locked it to preserve the scene.

When the bomb squad arrived later they started, to the McCabes' disgust, to break down the door instead of asking for the key. The bomb men were disappointed – there was nothing in the room except the note and the bloodstains, and there were traces only of what turned out to be gunpowder in the car. Forensic evidence, maybe, but nothing that would go bang.

ON Monday, December 7, Bob Platt was taking a drive in his lunch hour from a concrete works on the western outskirts of Canberra. He was in Urialla Road, a semi-rural area favored for picnics, when he saw something sitting underneath a tree close to the road. Curious, he stopped his car and got out.

He found five plastic bags, but they weren't full of rubbish of the sort often dumped in quiet spots. It was a strange collection of hardware: tools, wires and electrical components. There were also hundreds of rifle bullets in various calibres ranging from the common .22 to .243 to .308, and twelve-gauge shotgun cartridges. Some of the bullets and cartridges were empty, and there was a bag of bullet heads, lead shot, and wads. It was obvious someone had been extracting gunpowder.

But it wasn't the ammunition that alarmed Bob Platt. It was the small plastic device the size of a computer disk. He'd seen a picture of the devices found at the mail centre seven days before, and this looked awfully like it. He left quickly and quietly.

When the police came they found something else in the bags: a list of names and addresses of people, including the twenty-eight to whom letter bombs had been mailed the previous week.

There were also three two-dollar blackwood stamps and three thirty-cent saltwater crocodile stamps. Investigators already had enough forensic evidence to convict Dunstan, but this put it beyond doubt. As long as the link was established with Dunstan, no defence lawyer could dismiss it as scientific mumbo jumbo, and no jury could ignore it.

It would be a year before the scales of justice weighed the evidence against Dunstan, but his fate was sealed that day.

COLIN George Dunstan, forty-four, was found guilty of nine of eleven charges relating to mailing twenty-eight explosive devices. He admitted making the devices, but insisted they were not dangerous and that he had taken steps to ensure they wouldn't explode. Judge Higgins, of the ACT Supreme Court, sentenced Dunstan to nine years' jail, with a non-parole period of five years, backdated to May 26, 1999.

In his judgment, Judge Higgins noted: 'It seems to be that the situation was encouraged by the absurdly complicated grievance mechanisms engaged in within the Australian Public Service generally, and the Australian Taxation Office in particular. He was not alone in being responsible for elevating a relatively simple workplace difficulty into an intractable and lengthy series of administrative and legal proceedings.'

But, the judge said, 'whatever wrongs the addressees may have committed, that could not remotely have justified the campaign of terror the offender planned.' Dunstan's actions, he said, were 'a product of self-pity and a desire for revenge' out of all proportion to the actions against him.

CHAPTER 7

The Gun Alley Tragedy

'On the early morning of the last day of the year 1921 the dead body of a little girl of twelve, named Alma Tirtschke, was found by a bottle-gatherer in an L-shaped right-of-way off Little Collins Street. She had been violated and strangled, and her nude body had been placed in Gun Alley. On the morning of Saturday, February 25th, 1922, Colin Campbell Ross, a young man of twenty-eight, was found guilty of her murder, and on the morning of April 24th he was executed in the Melbourne Gaol. Face to face with his Maker, as he himself put it, he asserted his innocence on the scaffold in terms of such peculiar solemnity as to intensify the feeling, already widely prevalent, that an innocent man had been done to death.'

WITH those words, a brave barrister called Thomas Brennan began the most terrible story he knew, and one that haunted him all his life. It was a double tragedy that had elements of the crimes and punishments that stick in Australians' collective memory ... the Beaumont children's abduction, Gary Heywood and Abina Madill's murder at Shepparton, the politically-driven hanging of Ronald Ryan, the disgraceful police work and trial-by-media suffered by Lindy Chamberlain, the public outcry for Jaidyn Leskie.

Brennan defied the rigid conventions of his own middle-class origins and the blind respect for authority that held sway in those days to give an unblinking account of how the police, the press, public opinion and political expediency hanged a man on evidence Brennan exposed as a farrago of falsehoods fabricated by prostitutes, thieves and police motivated by the promise of reward or advancement.

It took just 115 days from when Alma Tirtschke, a Hawthorn schoolgirl, was raped and murdered until Colin Ross, a Footscray knockabout, dropped through the hangman's trapdoor in the grim bluestone building where the National Trust now hosts corporate cocktail parties and sells souvenirs to sightseers.

It had taken only a five-day trial for a jury to find the accused man guilty in an atmosphere that Brennan – his junior defence counsel – had likened to the 'lynch law' of some American states, where howling mobs still killed people without trial, hanging them from the nearest tree or lamp post.

Two higher courts had thrown out appeals on the principle that, no matter how dubious the trial evidence might have been, a jury's decision based on that evidence should not be overturned. The Attorney-General of the day chose politics over process by contemptuously rejecting permission to appeal to the Privy Council in England – giving his decision to a newspaper without bothering to reply to the condemned man's solicitor.

Those few weeks, in which public opinion was described by a contemporary lawyer as 'inflamed as it has not been inflamed within the memory of this generation', greatly affected Thomas Brennan, then fifty four. On the April morning that Ross hanged,

Brennan stayed home and wept, one of his relatives told the author of this story. The lawyer with a conscience immediately started writing *The Gun Alley Tragedy,* a cool analysis of the evidence as compelling today as it was in 1922.

For seventy-eight years, the Brennan family has believed that the Melbourne legal and political establishment – to which they belong, ironically – effectively turned a blind eye to a monstrous injustice created by corrupt police, a cynical press and a gullible jury. In the year 2000, just as time has almost erased the once-notorious case from living memory, a Melbourne researcher revived interest in a hanging as famous, in its era, as Ned Kelly's and Ronald Ryan's were in theirs.

After seven years' work, he uncovered overwhelming forensic proof to confirm Brennan's belief that an innocent man went to the gallows. His name is Kevin Morgan, and he is calling for Colin Ross's conviction to be quashed and his name cleared. This is his story.

KEVIN MORGAN had always wanted to be a writer. But he could hardly have invented a story as extraordinary as the one that grew from a chance event in 1993.

In July that year Morgan, then thirty-seven, a former teacher and a keen photographer, started a three-week training placement as a student librarian at the library of the National Gallery of Victoria. That month the gallery was setting up a retrospective exhibition of Charles Blackman's work, *Schoolgirls and Angels,* and, as Morgan came and went, he studied the pictures, which had the recurring motif of a girl in a school tunic and straw hat.

The exhibition catalogue intrigued Morgan. In it, Blackman referred to the murder of a schoolgirl in a lane at Melbourne's old Eastern Market, on the site where the derelict Southern Cross Hotel now stands. The murder had happened shortly before the artist was born but in the 1950s his dormant fascination with it was awoken by the unsolved sex killing of a university friend of his wife's.

So, thirty years after Alma Tirtschke was killed, the crime moved one of Australia's greatest artists to create a haunting series of images.

And, another forty years later, the case struck a chord with Morgan, a neat, earnest man as meticulous in his work as he is in dress and speech. He went to the State Library and found two 'pamphlets' on the case. One was Brennan the barrister's. The other was by a so-called fortune teller, Julia Gibson, who used the name Madam Gurkha and was a dubious character who disliked Ross and shared the reward money after his conviction, leading Brennan to suspect she orchestrated false evidence against Ross.

Morgan wanted to know more. For two years he haunted libraries and the Public Records Office, poring over old newspapers and searching a growing list of primary documents, looking for clues in a case that fired his imagination.

'I began to recognise,' he wrote later, 'that what I was uncovering was a trail of conspiracy unprecedented in Australian history. I realised that this had not previously been gathered, documented or placed on the public record.'

He found public documents previously thought lost or destroyed. With hard work, lateral thinking and a bloodhound instinct, he traced relatives of all the main players – Ross, Alma Tirtschke, the police and legal counsel – and found private letters, documents and photographs. All of it not only supported Brennan's belief that Ross should never have been found guilty but that he was, in fact, innocent.

Morgan checked every detail of the picture Brennan had outlined, leading to the irresistible conclusion that detectives had assembled an ensemble of liars from the street and the prison yard willing to perjure themselves (for money and favors) and so shore up a convoluted theory that Ross was the killer. For no other reason, it would seem, than that the police had no other suspect and were desperate to appease political and public pressure with an arrest.

The key 'evidence' was given by Ivy Matthews, a street walker, and Sydney John Harding, an habitual thief and proven liar on remand for theft and under threat of being jailed at the Governor's pleasure. Both claimed Ross had independently 'confessed' the murder, but their stories matched only on those points the police had been able to give them – and otherwise wildly contradicted each other.

Morgan's most important find was still ahead. And it was to come by chance – adding another eerie twist to a story that has several of them. But that comes later.

Everything Morgan found until 1995 supported Brennan's carefully argued case that the supposed circumstantial and confessional evidence against Ross was so obviously fabricated that it was preposterous. But 'scientific' evidence suggesting that Alma Tirtschke's hair had been found on a blanket belonging to Ross, though open to doubt, wasn't so easy to dismiss. For a start, evidence about the hair did not come from such obviously tainted sources – the prostitutes, pimps and jailbirds who had concocted testimony against Ross, probably with police connivance. It had come from the State Government analyst, one Charles Price.

Price was a chemist by training, with no expert knowledge of hair identification nor of the then fledgling forensic sciences, which in Australia had barely gone beyond fingerprinting. But, as an educated man in a position of authority, his opinion – presented as irrefutable by the prosecution – undoubtedly carried weight with a jury that the trial judge had neglected to warn about the unsafe nature of the alleged circumstantial and confessional evidence put to it by Ivy Matthews, Sydney Harding and other obvious liars.

Even without a judge's guidance, it was possible the jury might have been divided about the truthfulness of the rogue's gallery of witnesses recruited by the police.

If Ross's life hung in the balance with the jury, Price's opinion about the hair samples would be enough to hang him.

ALMA TIRTSCHKE, known as a well-behaved child, was running an errand for her aunt when she disappeared on that last Friday of 1921. She was last seen (by credible witnesses) between 2.30pm and 3pm on the corner of Little Collins Street and Alfred Place, standing near a lodging house known to be used by prostitutes. She was carrying a parcel of meat she was supposed to deliver to a Collins Street address from the butcher's shop where her uncle worked in Swanston Street. It was only a ten minute walk, but she had dawdled for an hour, presumably window shopping.

Although there were several conflicting statements later, no one except the guilty knew what the girl's movements were after 3pm that day. Early next morning her naked body was found in a tiny cobbled lane running off Gun Alley, where Nauru House now stands.

She had been raped and strangled.

Colin Ross was only one of dozens of people detectives spoke to that day and in the following two weeks. Ross was known to police because he ran a 'wine saloon' in the Eastern Arcade opposite Alfred Place. He was a rough character and, weeks earlier, might have angered police by beating charges laid over producing a revolver at his saloon. But, at twenty eight, he had never been charged with a sexual offence, nor ever questioned about one.

Ross readily told detectives he had seen a child walking past the previous afternoon who matched the description of the murdered girl. This was likely, as reliable witnesses had seen Alma going through the arcade, past Ross's saloon. Then, as later, he firmly denied any knowledge of the crime.

Three days later, the girl's body was released to the family. Just before the burial at Brighton Cemetery on 3 January, a policeman came to where Alma's coffin was lying at her aunt's house in Burwood Road, Hawthorn, and cut a lock of her dark auburn hair, 'about six inches' from the scalp.

Two days later, on 5 January, detectives went to the house in Maidstone where Ross lived with his mother and brothers, and took him in for questioning for eight hours. He consistently denied any knowledge of the crime, and offered a plausible alibi for his movements, which was perfectly corroborated not just by his brothers and his girlfriend but by neutral witnesses who had, between them, seen him at the busy saloon and travelling home on the tram in the time when he was supposedly raping, killing, and stripping the girl.

On 12 January, after a week in which daily newspapers, led by *The Herald,* put both the State Government and the police force under pressure by clamoring for an arrest, Melbourne's most renowned detectives, Frederick Piggott and John Brophy, arrested Ross at his Maidstone home.

There, while Ross was in another room getting dressed to go with the police, Piggott picked up blankets in the vestibule and asked if they were the same ones he'd kept on a couch at the saloon, which he'd vacated on New Year's Day after losing the liquor licence. Ross called out that he 'supposed they were', without seeing which blanket Piggott was referring to. Piggott later claimed he was attracted to the blanket by the 'sheen' of golden hairs attached to it.

Ross was locked in the remand yard of the Melbourne Jail in Russell Street. He could hardly have imagined then that he would never be free again, much less destined to die three months later on the scaffold at the end of the tier of cells.

Meanwhile, police and the Crown moved with desperate speed, goaded by the public hysteria and political pressure whipped up by *The Herald,* which had accused the Lawson Government of being miserly and inept, forcing it to push up its reward to 1000 pounds, to which the newspaper added 250 pounds. The total was like a lottery win, enough to buy several houses.

Ross was committed on 26 January, and went to trial on 20 February. By that time Price, the Government analyst, had compared hair samples under a microscope: taking a total of twenty seven hairs from two blankets brought from Ross's house, and comparing them with a dozen hairs taken from the lock cut from Alma's head.

It was to be the first time in Australia or New Zealand legal history that hair analysis had been used to secure a conviction, but few might have predicted that from Price's rambling conclusions. His evidence was strangely contradictory, given that it was to be manipulated to such deadly effect by the prosecution.

The hairs from the blanket 'were not identical in color' with the hairs taken from Alma 'but a light auburn color' compared with the darker red of Alma's hair, Price testified, showing why 'expert' witnesses are viewed with caution by experienced jurists.

The blanket hairs were a different diameter from Alma's hair and did not appear to have been 'dragged direct from the scalp' but were probably 'cast off in the ordinary process of nature' he said – implying they were more likely shed by someone who'd slept on the blanket, and not torn out by a murderer.

As Brennan noted tellingly: 'Mr Price might, on the facts he deposed to, have been called as a powerful witness for the defence.' Yet, in the lynch-party atmosphere, Price's admission under questioning that he knew little about analysing hair was apparently ignored by both judge and jury. All that counted, it seemed, was Price's strange assertion, contradicting the thrust of his other evidence, that the two hair samples 'were derived from the scalp of one and the same person'. If one sentence condemned Ross, that was it.

In different circumstances, Price's muddled testimony would have been laughable. But it would take most of the 20th century, and Kevin Morgan's dogged curiosity, to finally prove Price wrong. And Colin Ross right.

By mid-1994 Morgan knew he had gone almost as far as he could with available public records. He had applied to study the trial brief of evidence kept by the Office of Public Prosecutions, but had been rebuffed: firstly, he was told the box of documents he wanted no longer existed; secondly, that even if it were found, he would be denied access because the law stated it be closed for seventy five years. It was, in 1994, only seventy two years since the trial.

He persisted, and was told the 'missing' box had been found, but that he couldn't see it. He then had to make what he calls 'a labyrinthine application', including testimonials from referees, an explanation of how his work was in the public interest, and an argument that the act's purpose of protecting 'data subjects' – the people involved in the case – no longer applied because they were all dead. 'Especially the main people,' he adds, 'because they were Colin Ross and Alma Tirtschke.'

The application was submitted in March 1995. It was not approved until late July.

Finally, on a Monday morning that August, he was allowed into the Office of Public Prosecutions library in Lonsdale Street armed with pencil, paper and a tape recorder. No photocopying was allowed.

He undid the tape around the cardboard archive box, gently lifted out the frail documents and started looking through them.

Almost immediately, he found an Octavo envelope, the words On His Majesty's Service printed on one corner.

Inside it were three cards with three hair samples: Alma Tirtschke's, the blanket hairs, and a sample of Ross's girlfriend's hair submitted by the defence, which had been caught in a Kafkaesque nightmare of being forbidden to call another analyst to conduct an independent comparison of the hairs, on the grounds it might damage the exhibits. This effectively meant the hair could be used to hang Ross – on the word of a confused chemist – but not to save him.

Finding the hair, Morgan felt as if a hand had reached from the grave. After a trial all physical evidence was normally destroyed. But, by a fluke, someone had saved the hair by slipping the envelope into the brief.

It was to take him five days to dictate the contents of the brief on to tape ready to transcribe it, but all that time he was thinking what to do about his discovery. It was one thing to find the hair, another to get around the legal and bureaucratic obstacles to uncovering the truth.

When he finished with the file, it was locked away again – with the hair included. Meanwhile, Morgan gave up his librarian job and, supported by his wife Linda, a teacher, he devoted himself to the case full-time. The couple decided that if he was going to write one book that mattered, then this was it.

The obvious task was to find out if DNA tests could be done.

The Victorian Institute of Forensic Medicine was one of few laboratories in the world that could attempt a specific type of DNA test on such an old, dry sample. First, he had to get permission to have the hair tested.

In 1998, three years after discovering the hair, and with the access closure expired, Morgan applied to the Office of Public Prosecutions. The public servants refused to believe the hair was in the brief because, they insisted, all physical evidence was destroyed. They eventually agreed that the hair existed and Morgan, by arguing that the case represented the 'very beginning of forensic science in this country', won permission to remove one strand from each sample for testing. The old hair was unsuitable for DNA testing, but a microscopic examination by Dr Bentley Atchison of the Victorian Institute of Forensic Medicine showed that Price was wrong: the hairs did not come from the same scalp.

Dr James Robertson, a world authority on hair identification with the Federal Police forensic staff, agreed to do further tests – but it meant getting larger samples. After much diplomacy with the Victorian authorities, Robertson conferred the status of Federal Police exhibits on the hair specimens, and they were released and taken to Canberra by police courier.

Robertson's tests confirmed beyond doubt that Price and the police were wrong and Brennan was right. As Ross had said fiercely from the dock after being condemned to death, his life had been sworn away by desperate people.

KEVIN MORGAN is a painstaking man. With footnotes and appendices, he has written 300,000 words on the case that has consumed him for seven years.

Along the way he has made some fascinating discoveries, none more so than the Bible Colin Ross had in the condemned cell.

The Bible, which a Ross relative uncovered in a box in a shed, holds proof that Ross had not just died still staunchly protesting his innocence – but hinting that those he blamed for his unjust execution would be punished.

He underlined verse after verse, marking lines pregnant with meaning and writing notes in the margin, referring to Piggott and Brophy, the detectives who built the case against him.

At Psalm 26, Verse 10, he underlined the words 'full of bribes' and scrawled beside it: 'This is our police force which our people think so much of.' At Psalm 31, verse 13, he underlined the words 'Slander of many ...' and '... take away my life'.

At Psalm 35, verse 11, he underlined the words 'false witness' and wrote 'against Colin' beside it. Then he wrote the phrase, 'Time will tell'.

Both Piggott and Brophy were to become superintendents, but they didn't die happy men. Within months of Ross's hanging, Piggott's wife died suddenly.

Then, almost on the first anniversary of the Gun Alley murder, his only son was killed in a motorcycle accident at Craigieburn. He wrote sadly under his son's photograph: 'It is God's will.'

Brophy was to become chief of the CIB but on the night of 22 May 1936 he was mysteriously shot three times while parked in a car in Royal Park with two women. Despite the seriousness of the wounds – to one arm, cheek and the chest – there was no real search for the attempted murderer of the state's most senior detective, a clear signal that the shooting was a domestic scandal probably linked to the husband of one of the women in the car.

In the ensuing cover-up, senior police – including the chief commissioner Sir Thomas Blamey – at first claimed that Brophy had accidentally shot himself with his own revolver. This was clearly ludicrous, and another official lie was soon invented: that he had been shot 'by bandits' while meeting an informer about hold-ups. The scandal resulted in a royal commission, Blamey's dismissal and Brophy's disgrace.

So much for Piggott and Brophy. But if Ross didn't murder the schoolgirl, who did?

Thomas Brennan raised two facts that still fascinate.

'It seems doubtful,' he wrote, 'whether sufficient attention has been paid to the evidence tendered by Joseph Thomas Graham. He is a cab-driver by occupation, middle-aged, respectable, intelligent and thoroughly level-headed. On Friday afternoon,

30 December, at about half-past three, he was in Little Collins Street, nearly opposite the Adam and Eve lodging house, when his attention was arrested by a series of heart-rending screams coming apparently from a young girl … They were so noticeable that Graham and a man on the opposite side of the street both stopped and listened, but as the screams faded out each man went about his business.'

A week later, the cab driver read of an appeal for anyone who had heard a girl screaming in the area. He went to the police and reported what he'd heard, but was never called to the inquest nor interviewed properly. Brennan wrote: 'An absurd story was told by Detective Brophy about making inquiries in the neighbor-hood, and learning of some child that had a reputation for screaming … When Ross was condemned, Graham went to his solicitor and repeated his story. The full court heard his evidence, but it declined to allow a jury to hear it.'

The cab-driver was a credible witness with nothing to lose or gain, and who didn't know either the victim or the accused. But he came too late, perhaps, for his evidence to suit the fit-up that Brophy and Piggott had settled on.

Significantly, the suggestively named Adam and Eve 'lodging house' where Graham heard the screams was on the corner where Alma was last seen alive. It was known to provide rooms for prostitutes and pimps.

Which makes one of the dozens of letters Ross's lawyers received during the trial all the more interesting. The letter, received on the eve of the execution, was addressed to Ross but posted to his solicitor.

The anonymous letter looked genuine to Brennan, and he reprinted it as an appendix to his book. It read: 'You have been condemned for a crime which you never committed, and are to suffer for another's fault. Since your conviction you have, no doubt, wondered what manner of man the real murderer is who could not only encompass the girl's death, but allow you to suffer in his stead.

'My dear Ross, if it is any satisfaction for you to know it, believe me that you die but once, but he will continue to die for the rest of his life.

'Honored and fawned upon by those who know him, the smile upon his lips but hides the canker eating into his soul. Day and night his life is a hell without the hope of reprieve. Gladly would he take your place on Monday next if he had himself alone to consider. His reason, then, briefly stated, is this: A devoted and loving mother is ill – a shock would be fatal. Three loving married sisters, whose whole life would be wrecked, to say nothing of brothers who have been accustomed to take him as a pattern. He cannot sacrifice these. Himself he will sacrifice when his mother passes away. He will do it by his own hand …

'It is too painful for him to go into the details of the crime. It is simply a Jekyll and Hyde existence. By a freak of nature, he was not made as other men … This girl was not the first … With a procuress all things are possible … in this case there was no intention of murder – the victim unexpectedly collapsed.

'May it be some satisfaction to yourself, your devoted mother, and the members of your family to know that at least one of the legion of the damned, who is the cause of your death, is suffering the pangs of hell. He may not ask your forgiveness or sympathy, but he asks your understanding.'

Whoever wrote the letter must now be dead, and probably his secret died with him. But for Kevin Morgan the case is alive, and he believes he can identify the murderer: Melbourne's own Jack the Ripper.

Time will tell.

CHAPTER 8

Survival of the Meanest

'He jumped out into the lounge room pointing a gun at everyone and going "Pow Pow!". It's a toy laser gun and he is running around shooting all of us with the flashing red light. We all had real guns with real bullets. We could have blown his head off.'

THE more things change the more they stay the same. In each generation since World War Two the Melbourne underworld has started undeclared civil wars resulting in a series of unsolved murders.

In the 1960s two fruit and vegetable market identities were shot dead and another seriously injured in separate attacks. It resulted in an international inquiry into organised crime and a story that still makes headlines as the *Market Murders*.

In the 1980s, after the Great Bookie Robbery, gangsters Les and Brian Kane and Raymond Patrick Bennett were murdered as part of an underworld split and a television movie was made about it.

In the 1970s the so-called painters and dockers war ultimately led to a Royal Commission. In the 1950s it was the murder of gangster Freddie 'The Frog' Harrison as he uncoupled a trailer from his car on the waterfront.

But by the year 2000 in Melbourne nine men were killed in

what appears to be a series of planned, professional hits and there has been hardly a sign of community concern.

Three men were shot as they entered their front gardens, one in his home, two as they arrived or left work, another was followed and killed as he left his brother's home, one ambushed in his car and another in a seedy motel.

Two were brothers killed ten months apart and all were known associates of major criminals.

One theory is that the underworld pecking order has been disturbed following the murder of Alphonse Gangitano, shot dead in his Templestowe home in January 1998. Another is that an Adelaide crime family has been expanding into Victoria.

But, as far as police are concerned, they are just theories that lack evidence. What they have confirmed is that the victims were all connected through a group of violent Melbourne criminals, but they don't know if that circle is responsible for the murders, or just attracts them.

In the homicide squad, Crew Two was run by a veteran investigator, Rowland Legg. This team was assigned four of the murders that appear to be gangland related.

The victims appeared to be stalked, all were shot at close range in the head with handguns and all cases remain unsolved.

Because they were stuck with the four difficult murders members of Crew Two were to give themselves the nickname 'The Headshot Team.'

'MAD' Charlie Hegyalji was always security conscious – those in the illegal amphetamine industry usually are.

He filled books with the registration numbers of the vehicles he believed might be following him, was always discreet on the telephone and chose a house that he believed offered him the greatest protection.

His comfortable brick home in Caulfield South is shielded

from the traffic noises of busy Bambra Road by ten mature cypress trees that form a six-metre high hedge so thick it has been cut back to allow pedestrians access to the footpath.

There is a 1.5 metre horizontal plank wooden fence that acts as another buffer to noise and, more importantly for Hegyalji, as a screen to stop possible police surveillance.

Near the front door a small white surveillance camera is trained down the six-metre garden path. From inside the house anyone entering or leaving the property can be safely observed on a video screen.

'Mad' Charlie lived in the house relatively secure in the knowledge he had done all he could to protect himself and his business from the untimely interruption of police or possible competitors. But, in the end, it wasn't enough.

'Mad' Charlie was killed by a lone gunman who used the criminal's own security fetish against him. The killer crouched under the first tree inside the fence line and waited until Hegyalji came home just before 1am on 23 November, 1998, confident he could not be seen from the street.

Hegyalji was picked up by a business associate about 6pm and they drank at the London Tavern, in Caulfield, the Grosvenor Hotel in Balaclava and Newmarket Hotel, in St Kilda. They met up with two other men for their night of drinking.

To an outsider it would seem like an old fashioned pub-crawl but people like Hegyalji are always on the move, conducting business in pubs and clubs, and avoiding set routines that make them easy to track.

Charlie and one of the men went back to a unit off Inkerman Street, St Kilda, just after midnight. Hegyalji rang a Yellow Cab from his friend's unit to take the short trip home around 12.40am.

When the door rang Charlie got up to go, leaving half a stubbie. Instead of being dropped off outside his house he ordered the taxi to stop about a block away from home. It was another security habit Charlie had developed. The theory was that if someone was waiting for him he could sneak up unheard. It was 12.50am.

Hegyalji opened the wooden gate and took two steps along the stone path inside when the killer, armed with a handgun, opened fire. One shot missed but before Charlie could react he was shot several times in the head.

Neighbors heard the shots and called the police but Charlie's obsession for privacy concealed his body from the police torches and the patrol car drove off.

It would have made no difference. He died instantly and the killer, believed to be a tall man with swept-back hair, was gone in seconds, running past nearby Freeman Street.

About seven hours later Hegyalji's de facto wife, Ellie, was about to prepare breakfast for their two children when she glanced up at the security screen focused on the front path and saw his body.

The security camera remained operational and should have provided the biggest clue in the case. But for all his security precautions, Charlie had grown lazy – there was no tape in the machine. The sensor light at the front of the house had also malfunctioned and Charlie had not bothered to get it fixed.

It is almost certain the killer knew he would not be filmed or illuminated. The odds are he had been a guest in the house or had been told by someone who had.

Either way, it was an inside job.

WHEN Hegyalji, then aged thirteen, arrived at Station Pier as a European refugee he said to his mother in Hungarian: 'Where is the Statue of Liberty?' He eventually got over his disappointment at not being in New York, but never forgot the gangster dreams of his adolescence.

According to his long-time friend and underworld associate,

Mark Brandon Read, Charlie always wanted to be a mobster. 'All he ever wanted to be was an American gangster in New York. Through his fantasies he ended up becoming everything he wanted to be, except it was in the wrong country,' Read said.

According to Read, Hegyalji flew to New York and waited outside an old nightclub reputed to be a meeting place for members of the Gambino crime family. 'He stood in the snow for a week before he finally was able to say hello to Carlo Gambino. He pinched Charlie's cheek and said hello back. It was the best moment of his life.'

But he was to become more than just a tourist in the crime world. Hegyalji became a violent young standover man involved in rapes and robberies on massage parlours.

In the 1970s he began to call himself 'The Don' and modelled himself on the image of the US crime figures he revered. But by the 1980s he found there was more money to be made by being involved in the amphetamine trade than robbing fellow criminals.

In the 1980s a bright chemistry student, Paul Lester, quit university once he knew enough to produce the best amphetamines in Australia. He was a sought-after 'speed' cook who was more interested in tinkering with electronics as a hobby than making money from illegal drugs.

But Charlie was the sort who wouldn't take no for an answer. He abducted Lester at gunpoint from a Rosebud street, then drove him, blindfolded, to a Gippsland property where he forced him to produce amphetamines.

In another cook in Carlton, the process didn't work according to plan and Hegyalji poured the sludgy and volatile substance out on a tarpaulin, allowing the sun to evaporate the liquid and leaving the amphetamine powder. 'He called it "sun-dried speed",' Read said. In fashionable inner-suburban Carlton, it went with sun-dried tomatoes. Police who dealt with Hegyalji said he was funny and, when it suited him, charming. 'He was always jovial but he was always trying to run you. He would ask more questions than he answered,' one said.

According to one detective he bought a book on police informing from the US in the hope he would be able to keep the upper hand when being interviewed. 'He was prepared to inform but only out of self interest. He would give information to expose his enemies and to keep himself out of jail.'

There was no sign of him ever working and he saw no pressing need to collect unemployment benefits.

But if his quick wit failed he had alternatives. When police raided a Narre Warren farmhouse in 1995 as part of an amphetamines investigation they found a hidden armoury behind a false bedroom wall.

Inside they found nearly twenty pistols, machine guns and shotguns, six cans of mace, false drivers' licences and silencers. They also found a computer printout from a national security firm that listed alarm systems used through Melbourne. A pink highlighter had been used to identify the systems used in police stations.

Hegyalji's fingerprints were found on the list.

Read said Hegyalji was called 'Mad' Charlie after he bit off the nose of an enemy when he was still a teenager, but when another criminal was given the nickname 'Machinegun Charlie' he became jealous and tried to persuade people to give him a more glamorous title. 'But to everyone he was still Mad Charlie,' Read said.

In the 1990s he was a semi-regular at the specialist Prahran bookstore 'Kill City', where he would pull copies of Read's books from the shelf and demand to know from the owner if the author had made 'a million dollars.' All the time one of Charlie's minders, a giant of a man, would stand in the doorway of the shop, silently watching his increasingly-eccentric boss make a nuisance of himself. In 1989 Hegyalji was shot in the stomach outside a house in South Caulfield and he later shot a man in the carpark of a St Kilda hotel as a payback. In 1997 he was involved in a gun battle with another criminal associate outside a panel beaters in Prahran. Both men were unhurt.

Hegyalji was charged with attempted murder and kept in custody for just over a year until he was released in July, 1998. The charges were dropped because, as in so many cases involving the underworld, witnesses refused to testify.

Charlie went back to his old patch of St Kilda and Caulfield expecting business to return to normal but, according to police, his place had been filled by others. The people who had been left to run his business were not keen to relinquish control.

He had to flex his muscles and, when he was drinking, loved to wave his handgun around in hotels, playing up to his gangster image. But Hegyalji was forced to stop carrying his revolver with him at all times because, inconveniently, he was increasingly being stopped and searched by police.

In the drug business it can be as dangerous to be owed money as to be in debt. Charlie was owed more than $100,000 when he was killed but the debt lapsed with his death. It is not a financial arrangement that can be listed on Probate documents. Detective Senior Sergeant Legg, prone to the sort of understatement that comes from years of dealing with underworld murders, said: 'There was a little bit of business friction and there had been some ongoing discussions over the debt.'

In the world 'Mad' Charlie inhabited all his adult life, business deals were never committed to paper and some contracts could only be enforced with a gun.

Police do not like to use the term 'professional hit', believing it adds glamour to a gutter business, but Legg concedes: 'That someone was hired to kill him remains a possibility.' Six days before his murder Hegyalji rang Read to wish the former standover man a happy birthday. 'I asked him how he got my number (it is a unlisted) and he said; "You know me, Chopper. I've got everybody's number." He said he had a small problem with a mutual friend but he said it was nothing he couldn't handle.

'He seemed anxious and I knew he had some sort of problem.'

Soon after Charlie's murder Read found that his wife was expecting their first child. It was a son. He named him Charlie in honor of his murdered mate.

VINCENZO MANNELLA was nearly everyone's friend – outgoing, generous and funny – but sometime during his life of wheeling and dealing, he managed to make at least one serious enemy. And Mannella moved on the fringes of a world in which it doesn't pay to rub the wrong people the wrong way.

His last night on earth started as a pleasant summer evening. It was 9 January, 1999, with the sort of balmy weather that encourages socialising, and Vince Mannella didn't need many excuses to get out on the town.

He spent the evening with three friends in a coffee shop in Lygon Street, Carlton, and, later, a restaurant in Sydney Road. Even though it was nearly midnight the group decided to kick on to a wine bar in Nicholson Street.

Mannella, forty eight, and married with two children, drove his blue Ford Fairlane sedan back to his weatherboard house in Alister Street in North Fitzroy, from where he was to be picked up by one of the friends to go on to Elio's Wine Bar.

He parked the car in the front driveway next to his wife's BMW and walked towards the front door. The sensor lit the front landing and a security camera pointed from the roof but this would prove to be no help as the camera had never been connected.

He carried a plastic bag filled with leather belts he had just bought, a packet of Peter Jackson cigarettes and his car keys. It was 11.45 pm.

A gunman, who either waited outside the house or followed Mannella's car, walked up behind him and shot him repeatedly with a handgun. Mannella fell forward, his head resting on the welcome mat at the front landing.

Police have established that the killer carefully planned his escape route before the night of the murder. He ran about eight hundred metres along nearby Merri Creek and then up Albert Street to an agreed pick-up point. He obviously did not want any possible witnesses to connect his getaway car with the sound of gunshots.

But if the killer wanted to leave the scene discreetly he made an odd choice of transport. Police believe he was picked up by someone driving a terracotta-coloured Pontiac Trans Am with an eagle mural on the bonnet.

MANNELLA was the sort of criminal who was big enough to make a good living but small enough to avoid constant police attention.

Detectives who investigate organised crime knew of him, more because he associated with some of the biggest names in the underworld than as a result of his own activities.

According to police, he was an associate of crime figure Alphonse Gangitano, shot in his Templestowe house almost a year before.

He also came to attention as a possible source of amphetamine chemicals during the drug squad operation, code-named Phalanx, into Australia's speed king, John William Higgs.

When Gangitano opened an up-market illegal casino above a restaurant in Carlton in 1987 he invited many of Melbourne's major crime figures for the launch. When police raided at 1.30am they found Mannella, Higgs and another major amphetamines dealer in the crowd. When asked by police why he was there Mannella said 'I come here to eat' while Higgs said he was 'Having a feed.'

Police say Mannella was a middle level crime entrepreneur, the sort who was always looking to turn a profit, and wasn't too bothered what product he had to move – or steal – in order to make one.

In late 1998 he became involved in a gang that specialised in stealing huge quantities of foodstuff. Police believe the gang hit two regional targets and Mannella was the man with the contacts to sell the produce.

Detectives have found he was a heavy gambler, and had owned or part owned nightclubs and coffee shops.

While he was well liked in his own circle and, for a man who didn't work or receive unemployment benefits, extremely generous, there was an element of violence in his nature.

He was arrested when he was twenty-one for carrying a dagger in his pocket and six years later was found carrying two pistols. In 1981 he had a savage temper.

The owner of a small coffee shop in Nicholson Street, North Fitzroy, told Mannella that he was no longer welcome to play cards there because, 'He was acting tough, carried a loaded pistol and drove a Mercedes even though he didn't work.'

Mannella drove to the coffee shop on 20 February, 1981, and three times called the owner outside to try and persuade him to change his mind but he wouldn't budge.

Mannella then pulled out a pistol and from a distance of less than a metre opened fire.

The wounded man ran down Nicholson Street while Mannella shot him a total of seven times.

Miraculously, he survived, having told hospital staff in Italian that if they didn't save his life he would come back and haunt them.

Mannella was later sentenced to nine years with a minimum of seven over the shooting. Like 'Mad' Charlie Hegyalji, Mannella went back to what he knew when he was released from prison and, like Charlie, he was owed a six-figure amount when he was murdered.

One of the difficulties police face in an investigation into the murder of a man like Mannella is that 'friends' can be enemies and that business deals are never documented.

Arrangements are confirmed with a nod, plans are hatched in the back rooms of coffee shops and interested partners tell no-one of their schemes for fear they will be leaked to the police – or, worse, competing criminals.

Mannella was definitely owed money and may have, in turn, owed others big amounts. For a man who drifted in and out of the lives of some of Australia's most dangerous criminals either situation could have cost him his life.

'We are exploring possible motives including his criminal associations and debt matters but nothing has been discounted,' says Legg.

Mannella had $500 in his pocket when he was murdered. The killer didn't even bother to take it.

RISING early was no problem to Joe Quadara – after all, he had been getting up before the sun for as long as he could remember.

Horse trainers, newsagents and people in the fruit and vegetable industry don't bother grumbling about early starts as they are a fact of life.

At least for Quadara, his trip to work would take only minutes on the empty streets from his unit in Toorak, one of Melbourne's most expensive suburbs, to the Safeway supermarket in nearby Malvern Road.

After more than thirty years in the fruit and vegetable industry he had gone from being a millionaire to a bankrupt. He had once owned a string of big fruit shops and was a popular and generous patron of the Collingwood and Frankston Football clubs, but interest rates and an over-committed line of credit brought him crashing down.

He had to sell his shops in Frankston and Mornington, his lavish Mt Eliza house and virtually everything he owned to try and pay off his debts, but there were still at least sixty creditors when he closed his doors.

He owed businesses from $2000 to $50,000 although all of his creditors would admit he hadn't run away from his debts and had battled to try and make good.

Even though his business reputation may have been in tatters, he was still acknowledged to be a perfectionist in fruit and vegetables, only presenting the best produce and providing the warm personality that makes customers want to come back.

By then aged fifty seven, he had become the produce manager at the Toorak supermarket and when it was taken over by Safeway he kept the job.

He had worked at the wholesale market and in shops nearly all his adult life and was known for his boundless energy and enthusiasm.

But recently he had not been feeling well and had yet another doctor's appointment for later that day. He had already been told he might need surgery for cancer. What he didn't know was that it was almost certainly terminal.

That morning he drove his green Commodore into the rear carpark and stopped behind the Crittenden's liquor shop.

It was 3am on 28 May, 1999.

Two men, both armed with handguns, ambushed him and shot him repeatedly before he could get out of the car. People heard screaming and yelling before the shots.

His body was found ninety minutes later by a Safeway truck driver.

NINE GREEN BOTTLES

It was seemingly a murder without motive and police are yet to find the answer to a series of basic questions such as:

Why would two men execute a seemingly harmless fruiterer in a deserted Toorak carpark?

What is it about Joe Quadara that would drive other men to kill? And why, at his funeral a few days later, did three of Melbourne's most notorious gangsters, including the main suspect on the shooting Alphonse Gangitano, the man who was at Alphonse's house when the murder was committed and Gangitano's former right-hand man, all turn up to pay their last respects?

Police have now established the two killers were seen in the car park the previous day in a dark, medium-sized station wagon. It is possible they believed Quadara had the keys to the safe and the yelling seconds before he was shot was part of a failed robbery bid.

But Joe Quadara wasn't even the purchasing officer at the supermarket so he didn't carry company funds or have access to it.

Detectives said he was a good fighter when he was younger and had developed a strong survival sense developed from three decades in an industry often connected with seemingly unexplained murders.

'If someone had put the squeeze on him the pressure would have been put on gradually and he wouldn't have been parking in a dark carpark at work,' one detective said. If robbery was not the motive then the killers checked the scene the day before as part of their plan to execute Joe Quadara.

But was it the right Joe Quadara?

There is another Joe Quadara, also aged in his mid fifties, also with connections in the fruit and vegetable industry – and with a more colourful past.

This man was named in an inquest as having prior knowledge

of the murder of Alfonso Muratore, who was shot dead in 1992. He denied the allegations.

Muratore was the son-in-law of Liborio Benvenuto, the godfather of Melbourne who died in 1988. If it was a payback, it seems the wrong man paid the debt.

GERARDO MANNELLA would have known in the last few seconds of life the answers to questions homicide squad detectives are still trying to find.

As he left the house of his brother, Sal, in inner-suburban Melbourne on 20 October, 1999, he saw two men walking out of a lane fifteen metres away.

Police say he immediately yelled 'No' and ran about fifty metres, dropping a power tool and mobile phone he was carrying.

Detectives say it was likely Mannella recognised the men or saw the guns and knew they had come to kill him.

He ran from the footpath out to the middle of the road when they caught him, shooting him repeatedly in the head.

Mannella, thirty one, had been to work as a crane supervisor at the City Square project and to a union meeting before going to his brother's home in the middle of the afternoon. He had not been in trouble with the police for years and his last problem had been for carrying a pistol seven years earlier.

Police don't know if he was followed to the house or the killers had been tipped off, but they were waiting when he left to go to his Avondale Heights house about 8pm.

The killers were picked up by a third man driving a dark Ford station wagon. Mannella, the father of three, gave no indication when he left the house that he thought was in danger, but one career criminal with a history of providing solid information said Gerardo had repeatedly said he intended to find and kill the men who shot his brother, Vince.

NINE GREEN BOTTLES

'It is most unwise to speak openly about these matters because if people take you seriously they will be forced to get in first.'
Dead men can't hurt anybody.

THE Esquire is a good magazine but a bad motel. It has about forty rooms and most nights nearly all of them are occupied by people who want cheap accommodation close to Fitzroy Street in the busy heart of St Kilda, Melbourne's equivalent of Sydney's King's Cross.

The increasingly fashionable suburb, where millionaires and professionals now rub shoulders with the street people, still has a few hangovers of its seedier past – and the Esquire is one of them, a 1970s building in Acland Street that has packed a lot of low life into its three decades.

Drifters, backpackers, runaways, prostitutes and drug dealers can all get rooms. Some just stay the night; others stay for as long as they can afford the tariff, never having the security nor the confidence to look for something more permanent.

Late in 1999 a man moved into room eighteen and made himself at home. He showed no sign of wanting anything better. For him the location was perfect – and at $50 a night the price was right.

He was a drug dealer and he turned the room into a 24-hour a day business address. There was no need to advertise. Word of mouth in the street is all a pusher needs.

Local police say that for six months he worked 'red-hot' and built a strong customer base.

The dealer had visitors at all times of day and night. One of them was Richard Mladenich. The fact that it was 3.30am, that one man was asleep on the floor, a woman asleep in a bed and a third person was also in bed would not have fazed the man who loved to talk.

When the door of room eighteen swung open a little later to

reveal an armed man, it was one of the few times in his life that the standover man and serial pest was caught short for words.

The assassin didn't need to break down the door – underworld murders are seldom that dramatic. The door was unlocked and all he had to do was turn the handle slowly enough not to forewarn the victim. Before he walked in he yelled the name of the resident drug dealer – almost as a greeting – to show that he was no threat.

By the time Mladenich realised he was in danger it was too late. When he stood to face the young man in the dark glasses and hood, he saw a small-calibre handgun pointing directly at him.

His experience of more than twenty years of violence would have told him that only luck could save him. It didn't.

Before he could speak the gun barked and the man holding it was gone, leaving Mladenich fighting a losing battle for life.

Many people would have wanted Richard Mladenich dead but, ironically, the man who pulled the trigger might not have been one of them. At least, that's the theory put up by those investigating the shooting.

Rather than the killing being an organised underworld hit, some police say, it was more likely to have been a botched job, in that Mladenich was not the gunman's intended target.

If the theory's right it adds a black postscript to the recurring theme of his short, brutal and wasted life: that is, he was the wrong man in the wrong place at the wrong time.

MLADENICH was a drug dealer, a standover man and a loudmouth. He was also funny, outrageous, a showman and a jailhouse poet with a sense of theatre. If Mladenich, thirty seven, was hunted down by a hitman on 16 May, 2000, then detectives have a big problem. It will not be trying to find suspects who wanted him dead, but to eliminate potential enemies from the long list of possible gunmen.

If he was followed then the killer did a professional job, as Mladenich had visited several other rooms at the Esquire before he reached room eighteen just before 3am.

According to former standover man, Mark 'Chopper' Read, Mladenich was 'a total comedy of errors' and 'without a doubt the loudest and most troublesome inmate in any jail in Australia.'

In 1988 Read and Mladenich were both inmates in the maximum security H Division of Pentridge Prison during the so-called Overcoat War between prisoner factions.

'Poor Richard fell over and hit his head on a garden spade but he told the police nothing and dismissed as foul gossip and rumor suggestions that I had hit him with it.' Read was never charged with the attack but Mladenich carried permanent reminders of it in the form of scars on his forehead.

One night in jail Mladenich grabbed his plastic chair and banged it against his cell bars from 8.30pm until 4.20am – not as part of a jail protest, but simply because he thought it was funny.

'He was never short of a word. He went to Joe the Boss's place and stood outside yelling threats. This was not wise and a short time later he was shot in the leg in what was an obvious misunderstanding. He kept yelling abuse before he limped off. He could be flogged to the ground and then he would say, "Now let that be a lesson to you".'

Mladenich was fourteen when he was charged with stealing a car in Footscray. He was to end with a criminal record of more than nine pages and twenty-four aliases, including Richard Mantello and John Mancini.

But while he considered himself a smart criminal his arrest record is filled with offences involving street violence. He was no master gangster.

His lengthy police file included a large number of warnings, including that he had 'violent rages that can be triggered off at any time ... he will attempt to kill a (police) member or members.'

One entry read: 'According to prison officers with years of experience they stated (Mladenich) was one of the craziest and most violent offenders they have seen. (He) is a mountain of a man who has a very violent and unpredictable nature. He must be approached with caution and extreme care. A tough cookie.'

Read said Mladenich had a fierce heroin habit from the mid 1980s. 'He would come into jail looking like a wet greyhound and then he would pump iron and build up while inside.'

Nearly ten years ago Read predicted that Mladenich would die young. 'The drugs will kill Richard and it's sad to see.'

Read, now a best-selling author living in Tasmania, says many of his old friends and enemies were being murdered because they refused to accept they were too old to dominate the underworld.

'The barman has called last drinks but these people won't go home and they just hang around to be killed. I have found that the writing of books is a far better way for your middle-aged crim to spend his winter nights, well away from excitable types with firearms.'

Former drug squad and St Kilda detective, Lachlan McCulloch, said Mladenich was one of the more bizarre criminal identities he had investigated in sixteen years.

McCulloch said that during a drug raid in Albert Park armed police were searching a house when 'There was this amazing scream and Mladenich jumped out into the lounge room pointing a gun at everyone and going "Pow Pow!". He has this toy laser gun and he was running around shooting all of us with the flashing red light. The trouble was we all had real guns with real bullets. We could have blown his head off.'

McCulloch said that while Mladenich was eccentric and

violent ('He was as crazy as they came') he lacked the planning skills to be successful in the underworld.

The former detective said Mladenich, who liked to be known as 'King Richard' but was also known by others as 'Spade Brain' and 'Mad Richard', had ambitions to run a protection racket. He stood over prostitutes and drug dealers but wanted to broaden his horizons. 'He wore this black gangster's coat and a black hat and walked into a pub in South Melbourne. He said he wanted $1000 a week for protection money and he would be back the next day.'

When he came back twenty-four hours later he didn't seem to notice a group of detectives sitting at a nearby table, sipping beers. He was arrested at his first attempt at the shakedown.

Read said one detective tired of dealing with Mladenich through the courts. He said the detective walked him at gunpoint to the end of the St Kilda Pier, made him jump in and swim back. 'Would have done him good too,' Read said.

As a criminal he was a good poet, reciting his verse to a judge who was about to jail him. He once was waiting in a Chinese restaurant for a takeaway meal when he started a friendly conversation with the man next to him, complimenting him on a ring he was wearing.

When the man left the restaurant, Mladenich was waiting outside to rob him of the ring. 'He nearly pulled the finger off with it,' a detective said.

He had a long and volatile relationship with many Melbourne barristers and judges. He was known to have stalked a prosecutor, Carolyn Douglas (later appointed a County Court Judge), to have disrupted Supreme Court trials and abuse lawyers who have appeared against him. He once chested a respected barrister, Raymond Lopez, in the foyer of Owen Dixon Chambers. 'It is the only time I have felt under physical pressure in that way. I thought he was as high as a kite,' the barrister was to recall.

'He calmed down but he struck me as the type who could turn quickly.'

He walked into one of his old lawyers' offices, locked the door and asked for money. At the same time he noticed the barrister's overcoat on the back of the door and started to go through the pockets. It was a stunning turnaround to have a client fleece his barrister, and earned Mladenich an enduring reputation in legal and police circles.

One member of the underworld said many were happy that Mladenich was dead. 'He was a hoon, a pimp, and lived off everyone else. He never did one good job but he would come around looking for a chopout.'

But, as is the tradition in Melbourne when a criminal dies violently, the *Herald Sun* newspaper was filled with death notices, including some from well-known criminals, career armed robbers, and an underworld financier dying of cancer and several others well connected in the underworld.

It is believed that Mladenich had run up drug debts with at least two heavy dealers who were prepared to write off the money. Neither was likely to order his murder.

The dead man's older brother, Mark, who repeatedly tried to help Richard straighten out, said of him: 'He was sixteen when he was in the hardest division in an adult jail. He wasn't allowed to be soft. He had to be hard to survive.

'I know about his record but when he was with his family he was different. He was good-hearted.'

Mladenich was released from prison only a month before his death and told friends and relatives he was determined to keep out of trouble. But, as usual, Richard wasn't telling the whole truth. Within weeks of his release he was trying to establish a protection racket by standing over restaurants in Fitzroy Street.

There was an incident in jail, shortly before his release, that left him with another group of enemies. The story circulating in some criminal circles was that Mladenich had stood over a relatively vulnerable young inmate in jail, unaware the man was connected to a powerful Romanian crime family.

When the young man told his family about Mladenich's humiliation of him, the story goes, they sent a teenage gunman to avenge their relative's honor. According to the story, the killer was too young to drive a car and had to be driven to the scene.

It is alleged he uttered the Romanian curse, 'You are the Devil and we have rid the world of you,' as he left the room.

But police are sticking to their less romantic scenario. They believe the young gunman went to the flat to either kill or rob the drug dealer who had lived in the room for six months. But when he opened the door and found Mladenich, he panicked and started shooting. If so, it proves the old saying about the dangers of having a reputation.

LESS than twelve hours after Mark Moran was murdered outside his luxury home, a group of his associates met in another house in the northern suburbs of Melbourne to begin planning a payback killing.

Even before the body was removed from the crime scene police knew they were in a race with the Moran clan to find the killer.

If homicide squad detectives were to get there first there was every chance the killer would be charged and, if convicted, would be sentenced to prison by a Supreme Court Judge.

But if the Moran gang won the race the sentence would be automatic – death – and there would be no appeal. Mark Moran, thirty six, was always the apparent white sheep of the family, the one who stayed in the background and kept a low profile. But on 15 June, 2000, the man who shunned publicity made the headlines, the latest victim in the underworld war known to have claimed nine lives since January, 1998.

Moran's natural father, Leslie John Cole, was ambushed and shot dead outside his Sydney home on 10 November, 1982. He was the first victim of the gangland wars that resulted in the death or disappearance of eight Sydney underworld figures in the early 1980s. It took eighteen years, but Mark went the same way as his father – proof that, in crime as in horse racing, blood in the end will tell.

If police had any doubts about the potential consequences of Mark Moran's death, they were to learn otherwise within hours. A close relative of the dead man snarled at detectives: 'We will look after this. You can go and get fucked.'

The Moran name has been well-known through three generations in Melbourne criminal circles and the clan's reputation was not earned with a pacifist philosophy.

Within twenty-four hours of the murder Detective Inspector Brian Rix of the homicide squad admitted police were receiving little help from the Morans. He further ventured that the shooting had 'all the hallmarks of an underworld slaying.' Then the normally taciturn Rix produced a remarkably long sentence.

'The indications are that he was out of his car at the time of the shooting, which means that perhaps his killers laid in wait,' he said.

Sometimes you can deduce more from what police don't say. What Rix didn't raise in public was why Moran had left his house for less than thirty minutes on the night he was killed.

Who had he gone to meet? Did the killer know Moran would go out and then come back fairly quickly?

It is fair to conclude that an armed killer would not sit outside a luxury house in a luxury street all night on the off chance the target would venture out. Unless he happened to follow Moran back to the house after seeing him elsewhere he had to have inside knowledge.

So the real question became: 'Who set him up?'

Police tried to use the underworld anger to try and help solve the murder. They were the hunters on horseback chasing the hounds who were chasing the fox.

If they timed it well, the hounds would take them to the fox. If they didn't the hounds would tear it apart first.

As Rix said: 'Mark fancied himself as a bit of a heavy. I would think the underworld will talk about this to somebody, and I'm sure that will get back to us in some way.'

But he acknowledged the dangers. 'It's a real concern that they'll go out and try and seek retribution, but we've got to try to get to the family and say that is not the way to go about things … they've got to trust the system.'

The basic facts are that Moran left his million-dollar home in Combermere Street, Aberfeldie, near Essendon, for just over twenty minutes. When he returned a gunman shot him as he got out of his late-model Commodore. The shotgun blast knocked him back into the car, killing him instantly.

It was no surprise when it became known that a Moran had been murdered. The surprise was that it was Mark and not his elder half-brother, Jason, the notorious gangster serving two years and six months over an assault in King Street, Melbourne.

Jason Moran was a close associate of Alphonse Gangitano. The two men were both facing charges over the King Street brawl, but Gangitano was murdered before the trial.

It is believed that Gangitano and Moran fell out 'very shortly' before Gangitano was murdered. Very shortly, perhaps.

While Jason Moran was seen as wild, violent and erratic, his younger half-brother was calmer and tried to keep a lower profile. 'Jason was out of control, Mark was the brains,' said one policeman who has investigated the family.

But as Jason became increasingly restrained by court action and stints in jail, Mark began to assume a higher profile.

About eighteen months before his death, he took offence when an associate made a disparaging comment about a female relative.

'He went around to the guy's house, stuck a gun in his mouth, took him away and seriously flogged him,' a criminal source said.

Last year, he was involved in assaulting a policeman at Flemington Racecourse on Oaks Day.

About six months before Mark's death the Moran brothers had a falling out with a father-son team who produced amphetamines. The dispute was over a failed speed lab.

As is the norm in this world the dispute was handled with firearms. A women heard an argument in a Broadmeadows location followed by a man crying out, 'No, Jason.'

The result was the son was shot in the stomach, a wound that apparently caused a form of amnesia, because the victim could not later assist police in finding out how the bullet got there.

Detectives believe the Moran brothers claimed the father-son team owed them $400,000. They believe that Mark pulled the trigger.

On 17 February, 2000, police noticed Mark Moran driving a luxury car. When they opened the boot of the rented car, they found a high-tech handgun equipped with a silencer and a laser sight. They also found a large number of amphetamine pills that had been stamped through a pill press to appear as ecstasy tablets.

In a raid the day after Mark's murder police raided an associate's home and seized another five thousand tablets similar to those found in the boot of the hire car. Months before Moran's death he was ejected from the County Court after trying to use a false name to get into the plea hearing after his brother was found guilty over the King Street assault. AFL footballer Wayne Carey gave character evidence for Jason Moran, for reasons that remain unclear.

Police said Moran was one of the new breed involved in drug

trafficking known as the 'Bollinger Dealers', who associated with minor celebrities and the new rich.

They wore designer suits and used a pill press to stamp their amphetamine products to look like party drugs such as ecstasy.

Mark was a former professional chef and a 'gym rat' who was often seen at the Underworld fitness centre in Melbourne. He once listed his occupation as personal trainer.

But he had not worked regularly for years and police say his high-income lifestyle and magnificent home could have only been supported through illegal activities. He refused to speak about business on telephones and rarely spoke with associates in his house because he feared he was being bugged by police.

He was extremely proud of his fitness levels and physique and was described 'extremely narcissistic'. He was well dressed and when he was shot he was wearing a huge diamond stud in his left ear.

Mark Moran was young, good-looking, rich and extremely fit. But in the months leading up to his murder he was depressed and at one point hospitalised when he told friends he was considering suicide.

The day before Moran's murder police conducted a series of raids on a sophisticated amphetamines network and a number of criminals, including one known as 'The Penguin', were arrested.

One theory police are looking at is that someone connected with the network wrongly blamed Mark Moran for having informed on them to try to remove a competing drug syndicate.

A second underworld rumor was that he was considered an easier target to kill, because Jason was in jail and unable to fight back.

A third source suggested that a gangster with a grudge against Mark ordered the murder after warning him he was on thin ice.

But the favorite early theory was that it was a payback by the father-son 'speed' team and certainly that was the one the Moran family seemed to believe, at least initially. The favourites had good alibis for the night in question. While this may have impressed the police it left associates of the Morans unconvinced.

Within days of the murder there were reports of shots fired near the North Fitzroy family home of the main suspects.

Police sources said they were concerned for the welfare of a lawyer who regularly socialises with several members of the Moran family.

'It is not the right time to be taking sides,' a detective said last night.

The *Herald Sun*, the underworld's newspaper of record, was filled with death notices to a 'lovely gentleman'. There were many from former league footballers including one from a colourful former Carlton captain who fondly remembering them running a victory lap after a premiership in the 1980s.

There was one notice falsely placed under the nick-name of a drug squad detective. Police suspect it was placed to give the appearance Moran was talking to police when he was killed.

The funeral was the usual procession of real friends, hangers-on, crims in black suits who refused to take their sunglasses off, even though it was a cold winter's day, and bikies who would not take their colours off, even when inside the church.

Jason Moran was allowed day leave from prison to speak at the funeral. Mourners said the brother spoke with real emotion but his death notice concerned police. It read: 'This is only the beginning, it will never be the end. REMEMBER, I WILL NEVER FORGET.'

Some mourners were less than impressed when a long-haired Hells Angel insisted on embracing Jason inside the church. 'You should never touch someone on day leave.

What if the screws think you've slipped him something,' said a mourner with plenty of jail time. Because the funeral was going to choke local streets a request was made for uniformed police to control traffic but a senior policeman vetoed the plan. He didn't want media images of police holding up traffic for some of Australia's most dangerous gangsters and their hangers on.

While Mark Moran had a low public profile police had no doubt he had a long, and violent, criminal history.

Career criminal Raymond John Denning once told an inquest that Moran was one of three men involved in an armed robbery where a guard was shot dead.

He said the other two men involved were the notorious Russell 'Mad Dog' Cox and Santo Mercuri.

The robbery occurred on 11 July, 1988, in Barkly Square, Brunswick. Two armed guards leaving the Coles warehouse with a cash tin were held up at gunpoint. A struggle followed and Dominik Hefti, thirty one, was shot in the chest and the leg. He died two days later at the Royal Melbourne Hospital.

Denning said the three men planned to kill a woman whose car Mercuri had stolen for his getaway. Denning said: 'It was decided among the three of them that they try to find her home address and knock her because she was the only one that Sam believed had identified him.'

Senior Sergeant Peter Butts, formerly of the armed robbery squad, said that when police later raided Russell Cox's Doncaster home, they found that the the page of the telephone book carrying the woman's name and address had been torn out. Hefti's murder sparked another spate of killings. Police wrongly believed that an armed robber called Graeme Jensen was responsible and he was shot during an attempt to arrest him on 11 October, 1988.

The following day two young police constables, Steven Tynan and Damian Eyre, were murdered in Walsh Street, South Yarra, as a payback. It was the biggest outrage against Victoria's police since the Stringybark Creek shootings by the Kelly Gang in the 1870s. Mark Read had predicted only weeks before Moran's shooting there would soon be another murder.

'It is heating up quite nicely at the moment and it is a long way from finished. It is a good time to be retired,' he said at the time.

Police said that in nearly all the underworld murders since 1998 the killers had either stalked their victims or had inside knowledge of their movements.

Police do not know if all the murders are linked but they have been able to find that nearly all the victims knew each other. Interestingly, many were invited to the opening of Alphonse Gangitano's illegal casino in 1987. Which proves, if nothing else, that it's a small world.

There's another postscript to the Moran murder. In their idle moments, detectives and others interested in the case wonder if there might be a link between the murder and the unsolved killing of Frank Benvenuto, shot dead in Beaumaris on 8 May, 2000. Benvenuto was the son of the former Godfather of Melbourne, Liborio Benvenuto, one of the fortunate people in his field to die of natural causes, which he did on 10 June, 1988.

Moran and Frank Benvenuto were what police call 'known associates', which is not always the same thing as lifelong friends. Moran was killed with a shotgun, the preferred weapon in Italian payback killings. Although, as any member of the largely law-abiding Italian community would point out, shotguns are very common weapons.

UNSOLVED UNDERWORLD MURDER VICTIMS:

VICTIM: **Alphonse John Gangitano.**
DETAIL: Shot dead in his Templestowe home on
16 January 1998.
MOTIVE: Falling out with former friend.

VICTIM: *Mad Charlie Hegyalji.*
DETAIL: *Shot dead in front garden of his
South Caulfield home on 23 November, 1998.*
MOTIVE: *Possibly debt or drug related.*

VICTIM: **Vince Mannella.**
DETAIL: Shot as he returned to his North Fitzroy
home on 9 January, 1999.
MOTIVE: Possibly debt related or connected with an
underworld power struggle.

VICTIM: *Joe Quadara.*
DETAIL: *Shot dead as he arrived at work at a
Toorak supermarket on 3am on 28 May, 1999.*
MOTIVE: *Unknown, possibly armed robbery gone wrong.*

VICTIM: **Dimitrios Belias.**
DETAIL: Found by cleaners in a pool of blood below
a St Kilda Road office on 9 September, 1999.
MOTIVE: Failure to pay gambling debt.

VICTIM: *Gerardo Mannella.*
DETAIL: *Shot dead as he left his brother's North Fitzroy
home on 20 October, 1999.*
MOTIVE: *Possibly pre-emptive strike because the killers
believed he planned to avenge his brother's murder.*

VICTIM: **Frank Benvenuto.**
DETAIL: Shot dead in Beaumaris on 8 May, 2000
MOTIVE: Debt related.

*VICTIM: **Richard Mladenich.***
*DETAIL: Shot dead while visiting a friend in a St Kilda
          motel on 16 May, 2000.*
MOTIVE: Possible mistaken identity.

VICTIM: **Mark Moran.**
DETAIL: Shot dead outside his luxury home near
         Essendon on 15 June, 2000.
MOTIVE: Possible payback for earlier shooting.

CHAPTER 9

Yesterday's Man

'He ended up getting four years. We got life.'

CALL him Ross Stephens. It's not his real name, just another one of the aliases he'll need for the rest of his life. It takes a bit to surprise a man who's been through what 'Stephens' has, but when the phone rang at 3am in the upstairs main bedroom of a nondescript rented house in a town near Manchester, England, he was surprised, all right. Not only by the unearthly hour – but by the fact it rang at all. Only about a dozen people on earth knew how to contact him, and then only in an emergency.

The man on the other end of the line was a senior policeman on the other side of the world, in Melbourne, with a message that couldn't wait for a more civilised hour.

His name was Superintendent Peter Halloran, and he was in charge of witness protection for the Victoria Police. The call was short and grim.

'He said: "You have to get out of the house immediately. You have been compromised",' a disillusioned Stephens was to recall later.

Stephens wasn't happy, but he didn't argue. He knew Halloran was not the type to over-react. The policeman with more than twenty five years practical experience never took a backward step and was not prone to exaggeration. If he judged that being 'compromised' was a matter of life and death, then Stephens accepted it.

That didn't mean he had to like it. He put the handpiece back in the cradle, composed himself, and woke his wife, their two sons and visiting mother-in-law, packed a few possessions and ordered a cab to take them to the railway station.

And he did something that had become second nature to him over the previous five years when talking to his family.

He lied.

This time he told them they needed to leave the country for a few days because their permanent resident status had finally come through and they could now re-enter Britain as immigrants rather than visitors.

On the train to London the rest of the family chatted, happy that their future appeared to be finally secure. But Stephens was quiet, still thinking of Halloran's call and what it really meant.

Not that he needed to dwell on it. He knew all too well that he was the most important witness in the prosecution case against Australia's biggest amphetamines manufacturer – John William Samuel Higgs. The brutal truth was that he had been moved to the other side of the world to keep him alive long enough to testify.

The case that had taken eight years to build would live or die on the sworn evidence of Stephens, a man who stumbled into the investigation and was later manipulated into giving evidence against a drug cartel that had corrupt police on its payroll.

Now, in one of the biggest security breaches in policing, the electronically-protected drug squad office in St Kilda Road had been burgled in what was clearly an inside job. It was an appalling scandal of the sort that erodes the foundations of legitimate police work in a democratic society, and yet it happened just as blatantly as it might have in a South American cocaine republic.

The thieves ignored thousands of pages and hundreds of files stacked neatly on twenty-four shelves in three grey bookcases in the locked evidence room. There was no attempt to disguise what they wanted: the blue binders that contained more than one hundred statements that Stephens had made on the activities of Higgs.

The thieves also grabbed receipts and bills that gave away the secret witness's not-so-secret address in Britain.

Higgs and the police knew that if Stephens was neutralised – as either a credible witness, or even a living one – the prosecution case would collapse.

The security breach, discovered in January, 1997, was not the first and would not be the last time that Stephens was to feel like a foot soldier whose generals were all too ready to sacrifice him as an unfortunate casualty in the war against drugs.

Over time he began to fear his enemies less and realise many of his problems were being generated by those who were supposed to protect him.

He was at risk of being killed by friendly fire.

BACK home in Melbourne, Stephens had been a surefooted businessman who could make money and lose it just as quickly. A smart, savvy man with an eye for a dollar, he would latch on to an opportunity only to become bored and let his work drift.

During these lapses his social life revolved around playing cards, often all night, and in 1989 he was declared bankrupt after a long, lean run. But he was a great salesman and whenever he was in financial trouble he would return to his core business of selling cars to make quick bucks. By the early 1990s he had climbed back to making business deals outside the car industry and buying and selling produce on an international scale.

Through an old card-playing mate he was introduced to a man who wanted business advice. Enter John Higgs, a middle-aged man with a past. The two first met at the Britannia Hotel in North Melbourne in June, 1992.

'He was involved in a fish shop in Geelong and wanted to get an export licence to sell fish,' Stephens was to recall of that first meeting with the man who seemed part motorcycle gangster, part millionaire. Higgs was also exploring the viability of exporting stock feed to Asia and, apparently, making several overseas trips to set up the business.

The two were to meet many times in the following twelve months. It was the typical transition from social to business to friendship that Stephens had developed with others throughout his adult life. But, being gregarious by nature, he had friends on both sides of the law.

One of them was Ian Tolson, who had been a policeman for twenty-five years, with more than ten of those spent investigating organised crime for the Bureau of Criminal Intelligence and the National Crime Authority.

As soon as Stephens told Tolson of his new business contact the detective saw the opportunity of tapping into a drug network that up until then had always stayed one step in front of the law – often with inside help. Tolson was a recognised expert in cultivating informers and, believing the businessman with a wide network of associates could be of value, registered Stephens as an intelligence source.

He was given a codename … E2/92.

The understanding was that Tolson would use Stephens to gather any information that came his way. It would be a long way from hard evidence but it could be useful. It certainly couldn't hurt. But he warned Stephens not to get out of his depth because Higgs was a heavy gangster – a man with a reputation for being able to make enemies disappear.

Stephens fronted Higgs about his past and the former bikie freely admitted his prior convictions for drug dealing but said he was now interested in making money legitimately. Then, in a meeting in early 1993 in Stephens' office, Higgs spotted some paperwork on the desk over a fertiliser deal with the chemical giant ICI.

It was enough to spark a new level of interest by Higgs in his new pal. The drug dealer had fallen out with his chemical supplier in Sydney, 'Kiwi' Joe Moran, over a failed amphetamines cook and needed a new contact. Stephens looked promising.

Within weeks an associate of Higgs arrived at the office and asked Stephens if he could provide bulk chemicals. It didn't need an industrial chemist to tell Stephens he was being asked to become a partner in the amphetamines business.

He went to Tolson, who was about to leave the police force to set up his own travel agency. The soon-to-be retired policeman put him in touch with Wayne Strawhorn of the drug squad – an investigator with a long term interest in Higgs' activities.

On 18 June, 1993, the three men met in a North Melbourne coffee shop. Strawhorn told Stephens he was interested in the activities of Higgs and would be grateful for any information. It was all low key. Nothing was written down and Stephens agreed to chat with the detective if he found out anything interesting.

As a card player, Stephens should have known that Strawhorn was playing his hand close to the chest. The truth was that Higgs was the biggest amphetamines dealer in the country and, significantly, had proved to be untouchable for years.

He had been targeted by the National Crime Authority,

Australian Federal Police and the drug squad since 1984 and nine separate operations into allegations from massive drug dealing to murder had all failed. It was a pattern that screamed one thing to a knowledgeable observer … and that was: Higgs had inside help, the best police money could buy. This was dangerous ground indeed for an informer, but the man they called E2-92 probably wasn't to realise that until later.

The drug squad started yet another probe into Higgs and his vast network in July, 1991, but it too appeared to be going nowhere. Only eleven days before Strawhorn met Stephens for the first time the drug squad, Detective Chief Inspector John McKoy, wrote in a confidential report, 'a concerted effort has been made to obtain a reliable informer against Higgs by targeting his known associates. To date detectives are no closer to charging him with drug matters.'

Then E2/92 dropped in their lap.

'He was a Godsend for us,' Tolson said later.

'He had an amazing network and was able to provide information that was useful to ASIO, Federal Police, Customs and the DEA in America. I still scratch my head and wonder why he did it.'

But, according to someone who knew the new recruit best – Stephens' wife, Julie – it was typical of him to agree to gather information. Not because of any noble anti-drugs sentiment, but because he was always looking for a new distraction or interest. 'I don't believe he had an altruistic motive. I believe he was attracted to the thrill of police work,' was her blunt summary, much later.

Years later, Stephens still doesn't know why he agreed to be involved. He shrugs his shoulders, smiles and says: 'It just happened, who knows why?'

Higgs was a leviathan in the drug world. When street dealers deal in grams and major traffickers move kilos, John Higgs talked of tonnes. In 1992 police were told his syndicate had successfully completed a $48 million amphetamines cook.

A career criminal with prior convictions for theft, assault, carnal knowledge, manslaughter, assaulting police and possessing cannabis, he was looking to monopolise the speed market. He would become the Bill Gates of amphetamines.

The one-time member of the Black Uhlans motorcycle gang bragged that he had taken amphetamine production out of the hands of bikies and turned it into an industry. Like the international diamond cartels, he even held back hundreds of kilos of 'product' to ensure the market was not flooded and the price remained stable.

He was relentless in his pursuit of base chemicals, stockpiling them for his 'cook', Brian Alexander Wilson, a failed New Zealand industrial chemist student who could produce top-class speed on demand.

Higgs moved truckloads of chemicals without problems, provided two hovercrafts for a syndicate planning to smuggle cannabis from Papua New Guinea into the Northern Territory and, like many big crooks, was involved in race fixing as a means of laundering black money as race 'winnings'.

When police finally moved on Higgs they seized $371,000 in cash, $415,000 in counterfeit US currency, properties, cars, guns and eight tonnes of chemicals capable of producing amphetamines then valued at more than $200 million.

Police were told that at one stage he had $18 million invested in Queensland real estate and was able to lose $600,000 in a failed rock concert without blinking. Police found that $1,733,439 went through his hands between 1982 and 1993, not that this was a big proportion of his actual turnover. At one stage he owned an ocean-going trawler in Eden, NSW, a fish processing plant in Geelong and a retail outlet.

He also owned a string of trotters and an excavation business and used a former town planner with corrupt contacts to organise building permits. One of his companies won a lucrative contract to remove soil from the Crown Casino complex.

He also had a horse feed and supplement business with connections in Malaysia and Singapore.

'Higgsy wanted to control whatever he did. He wanted to make a billion dollars worth of speed. Why did he want chemicals that could have made $580 million worth of amphetamines? He wanted to corner the market. He had been king for so long people always came to him,' Stephens said of him.

STEPHENS was to talk to Strawhorn virtually every day for three and a half years. Along the way, he became the single most important intelligence gathering resource for Australian law enforcement.

Operation Phalanx was to last eight years, result in 600 intelligence reports, sixteen separate task forces, the arrest of 135 people and destruction of the country's most sophisticated drug syndicate.

A police undercover operation rarely goes to plan. The targets are usually cunning, disposed to violence and often erratic. Usually, the inside man is a policeman who has completed the covert operators course. They are volunteers who at least know exactly what they are dealing with.

The police department maintains it has an obligation to the detective above the operation and will cancel investigations that get too risky.

Stephens, not being a police officer, was allowed to take unbelievable risks in unbelievable circumstances. In many ways he survived because he didn't know what he was doing. He didn't show fear because he didn't comprehend all the dangers.

At most meetings he wore a tape to gather evidence, even though discovery could mean death. Once, for instance, he was to meet convicted murderer Eris Censori in Brunswick. 'I got out of the car and for some reason I went back and ripped the tape out,' he recalled later. Censori met him with the words: 'Someone's been lagging.'

He took Stephens to a Brunswick park and stripped him to his underwear. He found nothing and Stephens went home alive yet again.

The agent was given a new mini-tape recorder to gather evidence. Detectives assured him it was 'state of the art' and 'foolproof.' He went to a meeting with some drug leaders with renewed confidence. As he sat there he caught his own reflection in a window and could clearly see the red light from the recorder blinking under his shirt. Horrified, he slipped his left hand under his shoulder to hide the light that would have given him away.

In Operation Phalanx the undercover was an amateur and the investigation just evolved. Decisions were made on the run and Stephens had to rely on his ability to think on his feet to keep from being exposed. As long as he kept Higgs onside, the others would follow.

Higgs surrounded himself with family and mates he had known for years. He was confident they would not betray him. But he needed Stephens or, more importantly, Stephens' contacts in the chemical industry.

Even as his associates were being arrested Higgs didn't want to believe the leak was his chemical supplier. He needed his new mate and was blind to the mounting circumstantial evidence that Stephens was a double agent.

Police supplied their inside man with tonnes of chemicals he provided to Higgs – utes, cars and trucks full of the stuff. Higgs could not afford to believe his golden goose was a police canary.

'For the last year and a half I wanted to stop. I had had enough, but the thing had taken on a life of its own. I don't even think the police knew where it would end,' he was to recall.

The near misses, mostly due to police carelessness, were terrifying. Once he was supposed to have driven to South Australia to pick up barrels of chemicals to deliver in Ballarat. He met his police contacts near the drop-off point. They were waiting with a Holden utility complete with the drums on the back.

'They borrowed it from a local dealership and there was three kilometres on the speedo. If they had seen that I would have been in trouble so I smashed it with a coke bottle.'

He said the rumour started to go around the syndicate that he was a police informer. One crook, Les Burr, claimed he found a police bug behind the radio of a car provided by Stephens.

'He was having coffee in Ringwood when they (the police) knocked off his car to fit the bug but when they drove back there was no parks so they dumped it about two miles away.

Les came out and reported the car stolen and the police said it was parked up around the corner and he must have forgotten where he had parked it.

Stephens said that when police learned the bug had been spotted they grabbed Burr in the country.

'They took him around the corner and he thought he was going to be flogged. Then they let him go, so he went back to the car – and there was a screwdriver on the floor and the bug was gone.'

Burr told Higgs the police were on to them but, amazingly enough, the 'King' refused to listen. 'Burr was a nutcase. He was paranoid and always thought the army was after him so no-one believed him.'

Stephens at times was on a high as he gathered evidence. Too high, sometimes. 'I remember sitting in Brunswick at the back of the old water works. I was with Higgsy's son (Craig, who was later murdered) and two other guys. We took delivery of thousands of packets of Sudafed (which can be used to produce amphetamines) and we had to unpack them and peel them from the packets. We were in a disused shed and the police had video cameras across the road. Sharon (Senior Detective Sharon Stone) said we needed some light and I said, "No worries. I'll burn the packets."

'Well, they were made of wax, weren't they, and when I put a match to them the whole joint nearly went up. You could see it from Sydney.'

He said two brothers under investigation through Operation Phalanx found a bugging device and drove to the Australian Federal Police headquarters and gave them the device. 'They thought the Feds were working on them.'

At one stage Higgs was sitting in Stephens' office when Strawhorn rang for an update. 'I said I couldn't talk but he said he needed to know what was happening. I said to Higgs "John, this is the bloke from the chemical company – talk to him. So they had a chat".' Strawhorn managed to pass himself off as the insider.

As the investigation reached a climax and many of the main players were being arrested, Stephens became convinced he was about to be exposed. Just as he was arranging to join the witness protection program and fly out of Australia Higgs rang, demanding a meeting. Would this be the final, fatal confrontation?

'I had to go. We met in a coffee lounge in Carlton. But he just wanted to introduce me to a guy who wanted to import pineapples from Thailand.' To the end he was looking for new deals, unaware that his career was over.

Stephens was in the drug squad signing statements less than forty-eight hours before fleeing overseas when his mobile telephone rang. It was Eris Censori wanting to meet him.

'I told him I was tied up but I had to go in case he went to my house and saw the furniture was gone. I got Strawnie to grab his gun and we met him in Punt Road.

'All he wanted was directions to get to Lakes Entrance. I got the Melways from Wayne and told him how to get there. It was all getting unbelievable.'

It was to get worse.

WHEN Stephens first got involved with the drug squad he understood he was going to be in the background providing the odd tip. But, slowly, he was drawn in from a bit player to be the star of the show.

'Higgs just kept introducing me to more people and that is why the net kept getting bigger. He kept telling me that when it was over he would give me a million.'

He said that in many ways he became fond of the number one target. 'He could be quite charming.' But he knew underneath it all that Higgs' rough charm disguised naked greed.

'He was buying these chemicals from me at unrealistically low prices and making a fortune. He feigned friendship to make money. He treated me as a mug from day one.'

At first Stephens loved the role of the undercover agent. Julie says her husband was always easily bored and looking for a new thrill.

The original plan was to try and catch Higgs at one of his twenty-two clandestine amphetamine lab sites, but 'The King' was either too smart or, more likely, too well-connected to place himself at the scene.

In 1993 he delayed a planned 'cook' because he was aware police were about to launch an orchestrated blitz against five motorcycle gangs suspected of being involved in trafficking the drug.

Without knowing it, Stephens rose from an informal intelligence gatherer to a pivotal evidence source. He had always been promised that his name would be kept out of it but it would prove to be a promise police could not keep.

A court decision in another drug case meant police had to hand over certain internal documents, including day books. This meant that Stephens' name would eventually reach Higgs.

Secondly, prosecutors said that the man who wanted to stay in the background would have to get in the witness box to corroborate the masses of tapes and documents gathered over the previous three years.

This meant that Stephens and his family were now in serious danger. Higgs may have been charming but he had been involved in killing a man years earlier and could afford to pay whatever the market dictated for heavy hired help.

Stephens says he was taken to the Office of Public Prosecutions in Lonsdale Street in March, 1996. The meeting left him angry, disillusioned and with the clear message that his welfare now ran a distant second behind nailing Higgs.

He said a lawyer at the meeting had implied that if he was not prepared to give evidence he would be left exposed to the criminals he had pursued. The meeting with the team who were supposed to be on his side lasted less than five minutes.

Several police involved in the case advised him to walk away from the mess but others raised the possibility of witness protection.

Although retired, Ian Tolson was called back for advice. 'I believed there was no reason that he had to jump the (witness) box. They talked him into it.'

Then there was a meeting in early autumn, 1996, that was to remain a sticking point for years. According to Stephens, a solicitor from the prosecutions office met him in a Melbourne hotel and brought up the case of Peter James Cross – the son of a former judge who gave evidence about co-offenders in a cocaine smuggling syndicate. 'He said Cross was given $500,000 after he gave evidence and that was the minimum I would get if I agreed to testify.'

Former drug squad senior detective Sharon Stone was present at the meeting. 'I heard the offer being made,' she said later. 'There was all sorts of talk of approaching the government or getting it from drug funds but the offer was definitely made.'

She says the figure of $500,000 was discussed by senior police. At no point did she hear anyone express concerns over the amount.

Witness protection in Australia is nothing like the movies. It isn't designed for honest members of society who stumble upon crime. With few exceptions it is used for minor co-offenders who turn on their former associates to avoid jail.

It gives them a chance at a new life.

But Stephens didn't want a new life. He just wanted his old one back. And there was one other problem. He had been a police agent for three years but he hadn't told his wife or children.

He had been living a lie – in more ways than one.

'JULIE Stephens' is an eloquent, passionate woman in her late forties who didn't approve of her husband's new rough friends and was determined to keep her independent lifestyle.

Having been successful in several areas of business, she returned to study in her early forties and embraced university life with gusto.

She had met Stephens when she was eighteen, living in Adelaide, and had watched him develop a business pattern of financial boom and bust.

She was still deeply in love with her husband, but she started to explore her own intellect and broaden her horizons.

'He is actually a brilliant businessman, a fantastic negotiator and has a gift for putting deals together. He would set up a business until it ran well, become bored and then take to all-night card games. He would neglect the business, go back to selling cars and then move back into management.

She wanted financial stability, so she bought her own house, a cottage in outer Melbourne where she planted roses to watch them grow. 'I would tell him, "I can imagine myself as a ninety-year-old here".'

She threw herself into university life and a new social circle while her husband began to associate with increasingly question-able characters.

When she queried his new friends – 'We had terrible rows' – he would snap that she had some objectionable friends that he had to tolerate. He said it was business and he was selling them cars. 'There was some truth in that. When Higgs had a car that had a flat tyre he would buy another one.'

She said she wasn't going to try and pick her husband's friends. 'Just because you are married to a guy doesn't mean you have the right to try and change him into what you want him to be.'

Some of the men who would arrive at her little home would frighten her. Of one, she said: 'He was an animal, I don't think he had any boundaries. He was capable of anything.' But she found Higgs always to be polite. 'Even now I can't say I dislike him.'

One day in early 1996 she was driving with her husband when he started to talk about moving to England to start a new business career.

Julie was horrified. She had lived overseas for years and really wanted to settle in Melbourne. 'I was having a great time and was more settled than at any other time in my life.'

But she began to think that she was being selfish if her husband wanted a new start, perhaps she should consider it. 'He was working six days a week until ten at night. I started to think about where we were going. I didn't say anything to him and I hoped it would all go away. It didn't, of course.'

He had planted the seed. A few weeks later he mentioned that he had been doing some 'work' for the police. 'I thought he must have been selling them cars.'

He drip fed his wife information over a few weeks, culminating with the admission he had been working on Higgs and the family might have to move. Typically, the salesman sold the move as an opportunity, saying that police would help set them up with enough money to establish a business.

They met Sharon Stone in a Greensborough hotel. Julie was furious with her husband for having risked the family, and she was hostile to the police who had dragged her into a complex and dangerous investigation without her knowledge.

'We wrote a list of what we wanted. Everything we said we wanted they wrote down. Nothing would be too much trouble. I said I wouldn't go anywhere without our dog and they said there would be no problems.'

Julie was to find that despite her strong character, her world standard tertiary qualifications, her links with the state's intelligentsia and her financial independence, she had been reduced to a chattel. Her future would be decided by police she had not met because of actions her husband had taken without her knowledge or approval.

She was now a dependent, subordinate to the wishes of her husband and virtually being deported from her own country.

'How could this happen? Do these people just get so caught up in what they are doing, chasing criminals, that they just don't care? We have been manipulated and I feel betrayed.'

More than three years after being unwillingly scooped up into the witness protection scheme she sits in a bad bistro in an outer Melbourne twenty-four hour poker machine barn and picks at a tired chicken salad. Worldly and bright, she still has no understanding of how police investigations work. She finds it hard to grasp that police can be as ruthless as the criminals they chase and that sometimes innocent people get hurt.

She cannot understand how her life plan has been ripped from her without her permission or knowledge and that, to the authorities, she is merely an attachment to a man with a code name.

It was late in 1999 when she slipped back to Australia to see some old friends for a few weeks before Christmas.

Few of them know her story. They are envious that she is able to move overseas. 'They think I am the luckiest person alive.' Some see her as churlish not to appear excited. They are hurt she does not offer them the opportunity to visit their new location.

A friend breaks down and confides that her husband is having an affair. Julie remains unmoved. She can't help but think that if only her husband had betrayed her with another woman rather than jumping in bed with the detectives investigating Higgs, her life would be much easier.

Julie says they have made new friends overseas. Ross is charming and affable. She can be cold and remote. She knows that at times she says things to punish her husband for what he has done. 'They must think I am some sort of spoiled bitch but I can't tell them the truth of why we are there.

'I need to learn to manage my anger. I feel as though I can no longer trust him. Every time he walks out the door I don't know what he will bring back.

'We have had some really black times. It has been intolerable. Even now I don't know how this all could have happened.'

AT FIRST, Stephens was given top priority. He would meet witness protection police in top-quality hotel rooms and at one stage he was guarded around the clock. A senior policeman told

Stephen's lawyer, Paul Duggan, 'As long as I am in control here we will not abandon him.'

Much later, the policeman would not recall the comment, says Duggan bleakly. Stephens says he was promised resident status in the UK and a green card to the US. Now he says that few promises were kept.

The family, including their two sons, who still don't know why they had to leave Australia, were to move through seven countries and were never allowed to settle.

Julie temporarily returned to Australia with Stephens to seek counselling for their problems. 'I still cannot come to terms with what has happened.'

Even though promises were made to Stephens in 1996, four years later he was still waiting. He arrived back at the start of March 2000 – police had said they would settle by the end of February.

It was to take another five weeks to finally settle their claim with the police department. Meeting after meeting was cancelled. The lawyers squabbled over clauses. The promised amount of money didn't eventuate.

At least one senior policeman thought Stephens was making outrageous demands. He believed the drug squad had become too close to their informer.

Police had spent almost $400,000 on him already and now he wanted more. Some police seemed to have forgotten that they had gone to him and asked for his help.

Meanwhile, Stephens was left in Melbourne – the very place he was most at risk. The day he was supposed to finally settle, the police cancelled three meetings.

Senior police had more pressing problems that day. He was yesterday's hero, yesterday's man and yesterday's problem.

Finally, on 4 April, 2000, he was asked to drive into the city to sign the documents. He did not have enough petrol to get home.

AS they sit in the autumn sun near the Yarra River, watching families rowing in hired boats and a dog splashing in the water, Stephens tells stories of being caught in the middle of Operation Phalanx.

He has the voice of a smoker, the accent of a man who has lived in many countries with a just a touch on English Midlands to it. Stocky with grey curly hair, he can become angry over his circumstances but, moments later, can laugh at himself. He is always mulling over his circumstances, looking for a way out.

What if I go public? Ring the Premier? Front at police headquarters to see the Chief Commissioner or walk into a suburban station and try and take hostages? Would *Sixty Minutes* buy my story?

But while he sits in the sun he momentarily loses his sense of bitterness at how he believes the authorities have betrayed him. He is back in a world where he is the star and a major police investigation rests on him.

As he tells his stories he chain smokes, hunches forward and unconsciously plays with his mobile phone. He laughs and shakes his head as he recalls the crazy risks he took and how often he was nearly exposed. He appears not to notice his wife sitting next to him as she stares intently, hanging on every word.

She goes to interrupt, to ask a question. He doesn't look at her and continues talking – he wants to finish the story. Her face changes as she narrows her eyes with a mixture of fascination and amazement.

It is clear that, even now, he has not told her all of what he has done. He believes she would not understand because he does not understand it all himself.

She snorts with outrage and ask questions that betray her naivete. 'Why would police let you do that? You could have been killed.' He doesn't look at her. 'It just happened. It was nobody's fault.'

She remains angry and sometimes wants to punish him for the way her life has been hijacked. 'We have met people who see him as really considerate and charming and they see me as a spoiled bitch when I treat him badly. They don't know why I am furious and I can't tell them.'

STEPHENS was secretly flown back to Australia to give evidence at the committal hearings. The fears that he would be killed were so great that the government changed the law to allow him to give evidence via a closed circuit link up from another court.

Police were considering using an armoured car to bring him to court after they received information that two motorcycle pillion passengers, armed with shotguns, were to kill Stephens as he was to be driven to court.

In 1997, when he was back in Australia to give evidence, police believe two detectives were followed to Southbank, where a private investigator photographed them meeting the star witness.

He was cross-examined for a month by seven barristers in 1997 before he flew out of Australia again. Associates of Higgs were still making inquiries in South Australia and the Middle East, trying to find where E2/92 had been relocated.

But, by 1999, Higgs knew he was likely to be convicted and agreed to plead guilty to conspiracy to traffic methyl amphetamines between 1 January, 1993 and 30 June, 1996. He was sentenced to six years with a minimum of four.

Stephens now wonders why police and prosecutors devoted so much time and money to catch Higgs, only to accept the guilty plea on a reduced charge.

'He was supposed to be the king-pin. The prosecutors said to me "with your evidence we are going to put him away for thirty years". In the end they copped a plea because it was all too hard. It was all too much.'

'He ended up getting four years. We got life.'

As an outsider Stephens was able to watch how the criminal justice system ran, and he didn't like what he saw.

He uses the case of former footballer Jimmy Krakouer as an example. The former North Melbourne footballer became an associate of Higgs and was burned badly by him – twice.

Stephens provided the information that put Krakouer in jail and he now regrets it. 'He was a very nice, simple man. He had given all his money from football to Higgsy, who lost it all.'

Krakouer, the former star player who had earned $870,000 on the football field, was broke when Higgs suggested he take some drugs back to Perth.

Stephens provided a Bluebird sedan to be used to take the drugs across the Nullarbor but the syndicate ended up using another car.

In January, 1994, police caught Krakouer taking twelve plastic freezer bags out of the door wells of the car in a Perth garage. The 5.3 kilos of amphetamines was only five percent pure, having already been cut by Higgs' crew from its original eighty percent.

While Stephens does not condone what the former footballer did, he points to the case as the way the system is a raffle. Krakouer, the messenger boy, ended up being sentenced to sixteen years – four times the penalty that his boss received.

'It was a disgusting sentence,' Stephens said. 'He did a mate a favour and hoped to make a quid on the side. Higgs was the boss and Jimmy was just the little guy.'

WHEN Stephens was gathering evidence he was vitally important to the drug squad. When he agreed to testify he was the jewel in the crown for the prosecution case. When the drug squad was broken into he was, for a short time, the highest priority in the force.

Someone wanted to find him so badly they were prepared to break into the drug squad and steal the files. If he was killed as a result it would destroy the credibility of the witness protection program, scuttle the case against Higgs and badly tarnish the reputation of the Victoria Police.

But, now the case is finished, he is like a fading and difficult pop star who can't draw a crowd. He is no longer to be indulged and no longer seen as worth any special treatment. People who were once available to him twenty-four hours a day no longer answer his calls. His request for police to pay for his accommodation while in Melbourne was rejected.

He says he has not been able to establish a new home and has not been paid the $500,000 he still claims he was promised to start a new life.

He has borrowed from friends and family and has been given $50,000 as a part payment from the police. 'Even with that they waited to the last possible day until they paid it.'

Stephens says he has been told that one senior policeman has deliberately slowed any possible settlement. One senior detective confirmed a high ranking officer had made disparaging and racist remarks over E2/92.

'He has never met the man and yet he seems to dislike him.'

At one point Stephens was told that money spent on his protection would be deducted from any final payment but the police department will not take into account that he was partially responsible for recovering far more than the $500,000 he claims he was promised.

Assets recovered from Operation Phalanx include the $371,500 cash, a large country property, several vehicles, $50,000 in toys and $30,000 in clothes. He even handed over cash provided by Higgs to buy chemicals.

Higgs and several of the main players in the syndicate pleaded guilty, largely because they knew that Stephens was prepared to give evidence. Lawyers involved in the case said the guilty pleas saved millions that would have been spent in protracted trials.

The irony is that the more effective the police operation is, the more expensive it becomes. If Higgs had not been successfully targeted by the drug squad then the force would not have to find the money to protect and pay for E2/92. While the court system was able to save millions because of the guilty pleas, the police still get left with the bills.

Serving police would be disciplined if they were to express their frustration over the treatment of their star witness, but ex-detectives are not forced to remain silent.

'I am disgusted with what they have done to him,' Ian Tolson said.

'He has been treated as if he was expendable. He put it on the line on a daily basis. He was in daily contact with the drug squad for more than three years. As far as I am concerned he was an unpaid employee of the police department and they have a duty to him and his family.'

Sharon Stone resigned from the force in August, 1998, largely because she was disillusioned with a department she felt had failed to be just to a man who had done more than anyone could reasonably ask.

'They have reneged on a moral obligation. They have used him up. I feel there is some personal jealousy involved. At least one senior officer has said he would end up getting more than he (the senior officer) gets paid.'

'If he hadn't given evidence for seven weeks at the committal there would have been a contested trial which would have cost a fortune. They won't take that into account.

'What they have done is just unfair and they can't or won't see that.'

The former Premier, Jeff Kennett, promised to investigate the case but lost government before he received answers from senior police. Senior ministers in the Bracks government were also aware of the case. But no-one has actually done anything.

Stephens and his wife were in Melbourne for all of March 2000 – even though they were advised by fax by the witness security unit not to come.

Senior protection police say they would prefer the couple remained out of the country for their own safety but, sick of waiting, the pair decided to stay until the deal was done.

Stephens says negotiations were protracted and perverse. 'Each time we got close they changed the offer. We had meeting after meeting. I want to settle this and get on with what is left of our lives.

'They sit in their offices playing with our futures. We are hanging by a thread. I just don't know why it all went sour. I did what they asked and now I am treated like the enemy.'

Stephens became so frustrated he talked of walking into a police station and trying to take hostages. He said he was promised $500,000, offered $400,000, then $350,000. He accepted in the end, he says, because he had no choice.

It may seem like a big lump sum but, he says, he and his wife were earning more than $150,000 a year before he became a police witness. And Australian dollars shrink alarmingly in many other countries.

He says members of the drug squad have attempted to help him, including one detective who has lent him $10,000 and later $5000 just to survive overseas.

'The irony is that he has been investigated by his own department for lending me the money when I needed it, while the official channels have done nothing for us.'

Throughout the world, police recognise there is only one way to judge the effectiveness of a drug operation. To check the price and purity of drugs on the street after a gang is smashed.

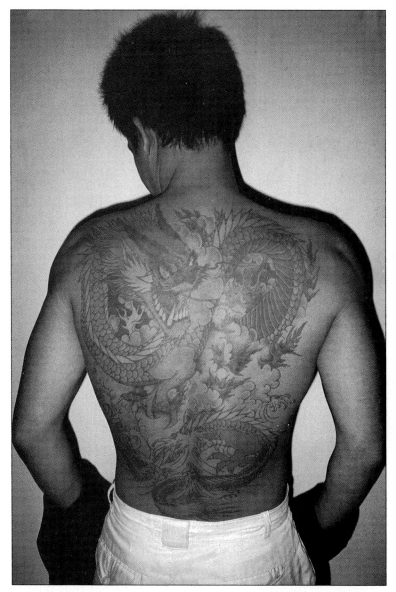

**Rat-a-tat-tat … this man will never stand trial
for an Australian contract killing because he has a date
with a machine gun execution squad in an Asian jail.**

Smoking is bad for your health … the Marlboro hat that police used to track the killers and the vases used to import heroin.

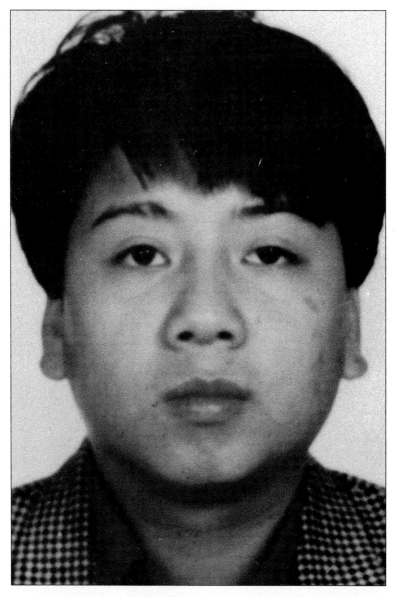

The victim … murdered in Melbourne by American killers on the orders of a Hong Kong crime boss.

Steve Tragardh with The Executioner.

Lunch in a Vietnamese prison … pondfish and dog. Yum!

Prison snaps: Australian detectives with Vietnamese prison authorities. Don't skip lunch.

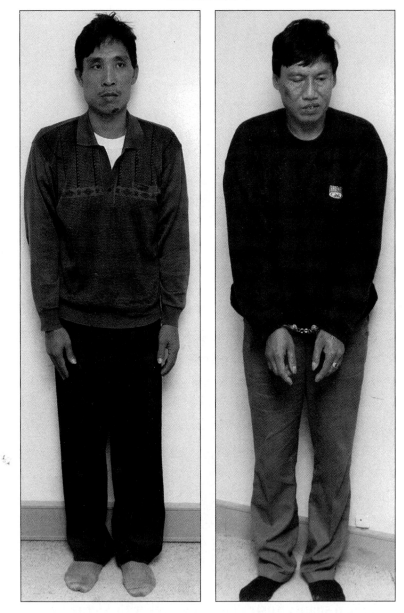

Brother Phuc's 'black pawns' … arrested while

trying to collect money for The Brotherhood.

A Hong Kong office raided as part of the
international police investigation.

Yummy. Brother Phuc about to get his last airline meal before landing in an Australian jail.

Not so yummy … the list of phone numbers rescued from a black pawn's mouth as he tried to swallow the evidence.

Richard Mladenich … survived a spade in the head, but not a bullet years later.

Another victim … Gerardo Mannella.

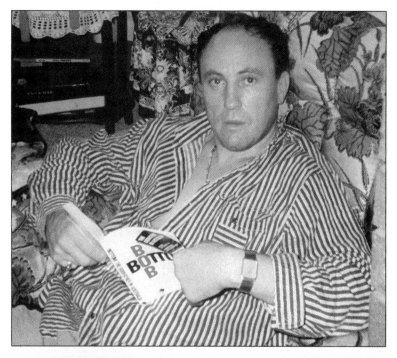

Mad Charlie … victim of an underworld war.

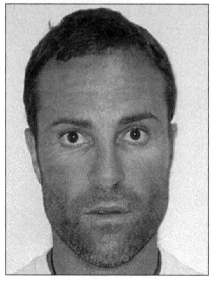

Death by shotgun … Mark Moran, murdered as he returned to his million-dollar home.

Big Ray Watson. A colourful cop.

Ray Watson talks tactics with a peaceful demonstrator.

**Jane Thurgood-Dove with mother Helen
and husband Mark at Easter lunch.**

Caught on film … the getaway car torched
by the hitmen minutes after Jane's murder.

Precious memories. Jane with youngest daughter Holly.

Colin Campbell Ross ... was the wrong man hanged?

When Higgs was operating, speed on the street was sold around five percent pure. After his arrest the purity dropped to between one and three percent, effectively halving supply.

Police who know what really happened say Stephens is a hero who has done more than any other Australian citizen to destroy a major drug syndicate. They say he and his family were manipulated so he was forced to give evidence and then squeezed to save dollars because he was no longer of value.

On 7 April, Julie and Ross Stephens flew out of Melbourne. They have lost their home, their country, their jobs, their future and their faith in the criminal justice system.

The same day the Victoria Police released a statement on E2/92 in response to media inquiries. It said, in part:

'The Victoria Police Force has invested a substantial six-figure sum of money into protecting this witness, relocating his family overseas, supporting and caring for them for almost four years.

'The witness gave evidence that helped put behind bars some of the most notorious criminals in Victoria. Police did not force the witness to give evidence in this case.

'The force has absolute confidence in the effectiveness and integrity of its witness protection program and the way the person was protected throughout the case. The witness was not enticed to give evidence with any promise of a reward.

'It is important to note that the witness has told police of the family's total satisfaction with the operation of the Victoria Police witness protection unit.'

Meanwhile, Higgs was in the medium security Fulham Prison near Sale – waiting for his release on 30 January, 2003.

He has passed on a message through contacts to Stephens.

'No hard feelings.'

Officer-in-Charge
Drug Squad

Chief Inspectors' Office
7th June 1993

SUBJECT: OPERATION "PHALANX". INTERIM REPORT.

SUMMARY

1.   Operation "Phalanx" commenced in July 1991 to investigate the activities of one Edward BESCHAY, a Melbourne criminal who was dealing amphetamine and U.S.A. forged currency. Through a covert operative, his amphetamine supplier was identified at Ronald Vincent FOSTER alias "Strapper" who was employed as a horse strapper and lived on a property and horse training complex at Lot 28, Dukelows Rd Mt. Cottrell. This property is the residence of John William Samuel HIGGS.

2.   Higgs is suspected of being a major amphetamine manufacturer and dealer. He was a founding member of the Black Uhlans Outlaw Motorcycle Club and donated their present clubhouse. He is also suspected of being involved in the importation of cocaine, heroin and hashish.

3.   Evidence has been extremely difficult to obtain regarding Higgs. He has insulated himself through a number of companies and apparent legal businesses and controls a large number of other criminals in his illegal dealings. Shortly after "Phalanx" was commenced it had to be suspended due to other commitments, plus the fact that other groups were investigating him. The operation was re-commenced again in August of 1992 with Detective Sergeant Strawhorn in charge.

4.   Since then a concerted effort has been made to obtain a reliable informer against HIGGS by targeting his known criminal associates. To date, detectives are no closer to charging him with drug matters, however are in a position to charge him with subornation of perjury and possibly conspiracy to pervert the course of justice over the early release of Eris CENSORI on parole from Morwell Prison.

HISTORY OF HIGGS

5.   <u>National Crime Authority</u> conduct unsuccessful investigation into HIGGS and one Gilbert BESANKO in 1984/85 for heroin dealing.

A confidential report into Higgs's drug operation admits police need a 'reliable informer' to tackle the syndicate. Then along came E2/92.

CHAPTER 10

Men in Black Hats

As Bui saw it he had no choice but to stay and be executed on the heroin charge. If he gave evidence about the syndicate in Australia it might save his life by keeping him in an Australian jail – but all his family in the United States would be murdered.

AT 12.46am on 20 April, 1996, a United States citizen about to head overseas walked into the North America Shop, a duty free store at the Tom Bradley Terminal inside the frantically busy Los Angeles Airport.

He picked up four cartons of Marlboro cigarettes and took $65 from his pocket to pay. He was lucky. Not only were the cigarettes much less than the retail price, but he was presented with two black baseball caps emblazoned with a red M on the front.

It was part of a special promotion. From 1 June, 1995, and 30 June the following year one hundred and fifty thousand of the caps were produced for duty-free outlets within the United States and on its borders with Canada and Mexico.

When he bought the cigarettes the traveller had to produce his boarding pass as confirmation. It showed he was heading to Hong Kong on Cathay Pacific flight 881 from Los Angeles. His allocated seat was 55B.

The man, Nguyen Hoa Ngoc, was not alone. In 55A, the seat

next to him, was Bui Quang Thuan, twenty-three, who was to continue on to Australia on family business. Bui's elder brother, another United States citizen, had already flown from Hong Kong to Australia a week earlier.

The brothers were on the way to Melbourne to kidnap and kill a man in Melbourne they had never met. It was nothing personal, just business.

The elder brother, Bui Tai Huu, twenty-seven, was not worried if the kidnap plot turned sour. He was a cold-blooded international hitman with prior convictions in the United States for manslaughter, drive-by shootings, and other violent crimes in San Francisco. His bosses knew he could be trusted to follow orders without question. In an organisation that required specialists he had developed his own niche. He was the executioner.

The Executioner had already visited Australia twice on business earlier in 1996. Both times he was involved in moving hundreds of thousands of dollars of drug money to Hong Kong.

He had a passport made out in a false name and in January had flown to Melbourne from Hong Kong, then travelled to Sydney, where he stayed for a week at the luxury Furama Hotel in Darling Harbour. At the busy ground floor reception desk he filled in his registration giving his address as Eastondale Avenue, Long Beach.

A few days later he was to meet his syndicate boss, Truong Hong Phuc, who had flown in from Hong Kong. Together they were able to collect $365,000 cash in the next three weeks. A further $214,000 was also transferred to Hong Kong and US accounts controlled by the group – known as 'The Brotherhood.'

Police were to find that Truong went to a house in Sydney with a suitcase containing $250,000 in cash. A few days earlier he arrived with a plastic, Grace Brothers bag. It contained $50,000.

TRADITIONAL Australian gangsters tend to be territorial. They may dominate a street, a suburb or even part of a city, but they rarely go beyond the borders where they were brought up. Some have become huge shoplifters in Europe or bar owners and drug dealers in Asia, but few have had the organisational skills or the contacts to control international syndicates.

But there are networks in Australia that are part of crime conglomerates with branches around the world. Organisations that can develop a business strategy in London to target heroin addicts in Bourke Street or King's Cross. Men who can decide from an office in Hong Kong to kidnap a man in suburban Melbourne because a woman who made a fortune in Russia would not launder the organisation's drug funds.

By contrast, policing is hampered by being geographically based. Local police worry about crime trends in their suburbs, while senior police remain concerned about state-wide problems. There are ten main law enforcement bodies in Australia, each with its own problems and priorities. Police officers have power only in their own jurisdiction – outside their own area they are just tourists.

But an examination of The Brotherhood exposes classic organised crime aided by modern technology and also shows the problem that traditional policing has in combating international crime syndicates that ignore national boundaries.

The size of The Brotherhood will never be known, nor whether Truong, forty-one, was its undisputed international leader. But what can be established is that virtually anywhere in the world where there was a Vietnamese community Truong, or 'Brother Phuc', as he was known, had real power. People did what he asked – almost without exception.

When he was in Australia, he ran up a phone bill of $6000 in just four weeks. He made calls to Hong Kong, the United States, Iceland, Russia, England and Canada.

Bui, the executioner with a huge tattoo of a dragon on his back, made calls to Britain, Hong Kong, Macau, Hawaii and Vietnam during the same time. For police, Brother Phuc was difficult to track. He would 'ask' Vietnamese people he knew to transfer money to accounts in Hong Kong – nearly always around $9000, just under the amount checked by law enforcement authorities. They would be paid $1000 for their trouble.

He would give them money to buy mobile phones to be registered under their names. He would then take them so he could pass messages throughout the world without police knowing he was behind the calls.

Brother Phuc ran his network from his small house in London although the drug syndicate operated out of an office in Hong Kong. His syndicate was alleged to be behind the massive importation of heroin into Australia, including a shipment worth $25 million smuggled in to Sydney in specially-designed metre-high pottery vases and a $4 million shipment inside Buddha statues and children's clothing.

Truong was small, polite and, in his own way, quite charming. He could afford to be pleasant because people seemed to always do what he wanted.

On 9 March, 1996, Truong turned up at a twenty-first birthday party in the Sydney suburb of Belmore. He was introduced to a couple he had never met and was told they were going to Vietnam the next day. He peeled off $10,000 in $50 notes from a wad held together by rubber bands. He asked the couple to take the money to his mother who was on holiday in Vietnam from England. They agreed without hesitation.

'Brother Phuc' then peeled off another $100 note and gave it to the couple's baby boy.

THE small and elegant Ha Que Thi Mai is an international success story. A woman who runs and owns her own businesses around the world, she had made it big from her base in Russia where she was living with a former Soviet intelligence officer. In

1993 her son, Le Anh Tuan, migrated from Russia to Australia. Her Russion lover unravelled after the abduction and murder. His relationship with Ha broke down and when he was brought to Melbourne from Moscow for the committal hearing he was clearly mentally distressed. From the witness box of the Magistrate's Court he gave the startling evidence that he was a Russian Tsar with the real name was 'Prince Bigdash'. He said he spoke seven languages, had studied law and medicine and if anyone commented on the weather it was a KGB code to make him operational.

He was excused from giving further evidence.

Ha was an entrepreneur, an investment broker with a PhD in economics, and involved in the high fashion world. Independent police investigations have shown she would feature in any Australian rich list if her assets were publicly known.

Brother Phuc would not have needed to see a balance sheet to know Ha was wealthy. She was to spend about a month in the Regent Hotel and another month at the Hyatt in 1996. Being rich was to become a fatal liability for her eldest son.

The trouble was, an international businesswoman would be a handy ally for The Brotherhood. The theory being that she could move money out of the country, and drugs, in through her clothing business.

Brother Phuc went to see Ha in the Regent Hotel on 16 March, 1996. He proposed a partnership to import clothing. He believed it would be an offer too good to refuse.

At the meeting Brother Phuc said the real deal was to import drugs and Ha was later to tell police she refused the proposition immediately. He told her to think about it for a few days and not to dismiss it out of hand.

At the meeting Truong made a cryptic and, ultimately, blood-chilling comment. He said that if Ha was difficult that the 'consequences for her family would not be good.'

For hundreds of years Asian organised crime groups have demanded compliance from others with a single threat: fail us and we will kidnap and kill your eldest child. It created fear in enemies and blood loyalty from subordinates who knew their own families were not beyond reach.

What was going through Truong's mind as he boarded the Cathay Pacific flight CX 104 to Hong Kong three days after the meeting will never be known. He might have believed he could force a partnership on the rich businesswoman, or he might already have been considering extortion.

Certainly, he already had details on Ha's son, including his address in Glen Waverley and his movements in Melbourne.

When Truong landed in Hong Kong he rang Ha for an answer. He didn't like what he heard. Stung by the rebuff, he demanded $400,000 as compensation for her stubbornness.

The threat didn't go away. On 23 March Ha was visited again by a female associate of The Brotherhood, and told to pay the money. Five days later her son, Le, received a fax at his home for his mother from the 'Happy Excel International' in Hong Kong. It was an unlisted fax number but Brother Phuc had no problems obtaining it. The document contained details on how the money should be transferred in $100,000 lots to four accounts in the Hong Kong and Shanghai Bank.

On the same day a Melbourne man arrived at Tullamarine on a Qantas flight from Saigon. He would soon learn that he had been selected to be the driver of the kidnap team.

Within a week police seized heroin valued at $3 million in Canberra. The package contained the address of the 'Happy Excel International Limited.'

By 10 April The Brotherhood was losing patience and the woman left a letter at the Regent for Ha. 'Sister Mai. I went to your place and waited from 3.30 for a few hours and you have not returned yet. You have told me to come to your place to pick up the money to give the other man but you did not phone me for the entire evening … I have wasted too much time. Whenever you return phone me immediately, I have no more time to wait for you.'

Ha instructed her son to withdraw $20,000 to give to an agent for Brother Phuc. But it was like tossing a fish finger to a circling shark.

THE KIDNAP victim, Le Anh Tuan, twenty-one, was born in Hanoi in 1977 and moved to Russia with his family after he finished primary school. He lived in a rented home in Moscow and, because his mother was already making money through her businesses, he was educated at home by a private tutor. He went to Moscow University to study linguistics before he decided to migrate to Australia.

He married as a teenager and fathered a daughter but the relationship broke up by the time he was twenty. In early 1996 Le was unemployed but had plans to use some of his mother's money to set up a clothing business. His girlfriend was expecting a baby boy when he was abducted. He was dead by the time the baby was born.

Late in April a woman went to visit Le at his Glen Waverley home and asked him and his pregnant girlfriend to go to Hong Kong for a business deal, but his mother told him she feared it was a trap to abduct him. But The Brotherhod could reach out, virtually anywhere in the world. Later, Le found that a spare key he kept in a rice container had gone missing.

It was never found.

If Le feared he could be the target of a kidnap plot he did nothing to protect himself. If he had gone to the police at this time it might have been enough to frighten off the circling vultures, but by the time police were aware of what was happening, it was already too late.

Around 11am on 29 April, Le went to his new house in Fiona Court to allow an electrician to install new light fittings. The tradesman didn't turn up so Le went back to his Regal Court home to ring him. Just over an hour later a neighbour looked out his bedroom window to see two Asian men chasing a third down the street. A green car reversed up the street and the man was bundled into the boot before the car sped off.

At the same time another neighbour looked out of her kitchen window. She saw two men punching a third who 'appeared to be pleading for help and seemed distressed'.

She watched as the victim 'put his hands together as if he was praying, begging for mercy, crying and shaking his head.' He was thrown into the boot and it was slammed shut.

Both witnesses called the police. By 12.35 the Glen Waverley divisional van pulled into Regal Court and senior constable Mark Standish walked up the drive to find the house locked.

When police went into the house they found a note in Vietnamese. 'You call mother to tell her that I have gone with the guys from brother Phuc's company ... those guys said to give mother seventy-two hours to pay the money.'

The deadline was set at midday on 2 May.

Who knows what would have happened if the two neighbours had not called the police? It is possible the money would have been paid and no-one would have known.

When police checked the scene there was little to indicate who the abductors were. But, as Senior Constable Standish walked up the drive, he noticed something on the ground.

It was a black Marlboro baseball cap ... one of the two given to a passenger who had bought duty-free cigarettes in the Los Angeles airport nine days earlier.

POLICE now know that three men, including the American hitmen, the Bui brothers, went to Regal Court just before midday.

The driver left the brothers, who used the key stolen from the rice container to enter the house and ransack it, looking for money.

When Le returned the brothers grabbed and beat him before forcing him to write the note.

They rang the driver on a mobile phone and ordered him to return. As they went down the drive Le broke away, knocking the cap off the head of one of the hitmen.

That night Mrs Ha called Brother Phuc from the criminal investigation office of the Glen Waverley police. There was no point in long discussions. The man who had organised the kidnapping said, 'You have three days to transfer the money to Hong Kong, if no money, everything happen to Ang (her son).' In another phone call nearly thirty minutes later he said, 'Look, I have told you already I can do whatever I want. When you have the money prepared, ring me.'

Time was already running out.

DAY ONE (30 APRIL): The kidnap victim was being held in a house in Glendale Road, Springvale. The kidnappers used four public telephones in Springvale to make nine calls to mobile phones used by members of The Brotherhood. Police believe they were given instructions and regular updates on the progress of their ransom demands. Police went to the Federal Court to get warrants to start monitoring suspects' mobile phones. The phone taps were to provide vital evidence but, ultimately, they would not help the kidnap victim. The tapes provided a chilling record, as the chances of Le living through the ordeal slipped away. Like a black box on aircraft, they were to show what went wrong and pinpoint when danger turned to disaster.

DAY TWO (1 MAY): Brother Phuc called the victim's mother, Mrs Ha. She pleaded for her son, but he made it clear that paying the money was the first step in any negotiations. He said: 'Now,

I am sorting things out with you now, and that is you owe me money. Are you going to pay or not? You tell me. Do not discuss any other matter. Everything has its place. You must sort out one thing first before you can go on to the next.

The $400,000 – are you going to pay me or not?

'You play games and there will be nothing good in it for you. Do you understand? You know my personality. You understand that? He will always stick to his principles, he won't cheat anyone, but no-one should cheat him.

'You better understand. There are still many games. I am not saying that it will be such and such. Do you understand? But with you playing games you have overstepped the mark a little.

'I have misjudged you. You are too low. I accept that I am stupid. I do not blame you any longer.'

The mother may have sensed that the chances of her son being returned alive were ebbing away and she started playing for time. 'I am only thinking of my child. But the time before I have already said to you to allow me until the end of May. But you did not understand me and did that thing.'

Brother Phuc remained unmoved: 'Why did you allow it to reach that stage?'

DAY THREE (2 MAY): Brother Phuc called Ha Que Thi Mai at 10.45am. He said '(For) the matter to be resolved between you and I if you want to be happy it will be joyous and if you want to be unhappy then it will be sad.'

There were further calls and threats at 10.57am then, two minutes later, he extended the deadline until that night. Later he again extended until noon the next day.

'There will be someone coming to collect the money. But if something should happen to my people coming to collect the money, then you will accept full responsibility. Everything is caused by you. You have brought everything about by yourself.

Therefore you have to accept the consequences. No matter how tough things get, you will have to bear the responsibilities … You have played one game after the next, In short, you can't win.'

Ha asked if her son is alive. Phuc replied: 'Now, you do not mention that matter too early okay. This matter, you sort out my money, that amount of money for me okay. After it is done then I speak to you … I promise you that I will take care of it properly for you. With my character of paying back in kind both vengeance and debt, do you understand? There … that is my only request. If you do that to my satisfaction then there is no problem … the money, if I collect it in full, all matters shall be happy … Whether you pay me or not is determined by your conscience. Everything, family happiness and the like is up to you to decide. I have told you many times, not just today.'

DAY FOUR (3 MAY): Brother Phuc extended the deadline until midday. When the money was not moved to the four Hong Kong bank accounts Le Anh Tuan, a young man who had been about to buy a house and have a family, was killed on the orders of a man he had never met.

In the days Le was held in the Springvale house he had refused to eat. Finally his kidnappers fed him sedatives and he was shot dead while sleeping. He was shot in the right side of the head – execution style – and would have died instantly.

His body was then dumped in an aqueduct in Mile Creek, Noble Park.

At 2.25pm, Bui Tan Huu, the executioner from Long Beach, rang the kidnap driver from the Melbourne Airport. Bui and his brother flew to Sydney that afternoon. Their work in Melbourne was done.

But Brother Phuc was still determined to get 'his money' and continued to talk to Mrs Ha. In one phone call the mother tried to draw him into incriminating statements. 'I am telling you the person coming to pick up the money is only a black pawn. You should remember that. The person is totally not privy to anything, okay? I have already told you that I am not going to say anything over the phone … apart from the matter of asking you to repay the money … Now, you do not have to talk to me on the phone any more. That's all.'

He starts refusing to take her calls. She rings and another man answers the phone, telling her brusquely, 'You do not talk over the phone. You cannot solve anything. Don't treat us like children. We are not children. You must understand, this is not Vietnam where you can trick people. Don't think like that.'

Later, she rang again. The man, believed to be Truong's brother-in-law, said: 'If you intend to play with the big brothers then you go ahead … There are people keeping an eye on you. You are not playing fair. That is why they do not want to phone you yet … There is someone keeping an eye on your every move. Don't think that things are so simple. You do not have to worry about anything. If you play fair then nothing will happen. It will be beautiful forever. That is all.'

DAY FIVE (4 MAY): Even though Le was already dead, Brother Phuc continued to demand the money. The following day the three 'black pawns' were ordered to collect the ransom at Spencer Street railway station.

Two of the men, including a former captain in the North Vietnamese Army, flew from Sydney for the collect.

Police now know Brother Phuc had some of his men watching the drop-off point and they identified some of the police waiting. But the man in Hong Kong was prepared to sacrifice his collectors in the hope they could still get the money.

At 9.28am, 10.26am, 11.07am, 11.25am and 11.40am Ha received phone calls from The Brotherhood in Hong Kong and was told to bring $400,000 to Spencer Street. She was told to take the money to Bus Stop thirty-one, where she was to hand it over to the 'black pawns.' But at 11.54am she received another call: 'You do not have to come. The way you play is pretty ordinary. You don't have to come … There is also someone standing there waiting for us already. You stay there. If you feel like playing games, then you go ahead.

'On your side, every move you make, we know. There are people there already … They have been keeping watch since this morning.

'You have been talking on the phone for a long time and they know what you are talking about. They have been listening on your phone. Happy or sad, it's up to you.'

When police moved in to make the arrests at 11.59am 'The Captain' was on his mobile phone talking to his controllers in Hong Kong. The three collectors were taken to the St Kilda Road police station. Police then noticed a bulge in the captain's mouth. He was attempting to swallow a list of phone numbers including Brother Phuc's Hong Kong mobile number.

Hours after the arrests in Melbourne, Brother Phuc flew out of Hong Kong to Vietnam and then back to his base in London.

At 12.57pm Brother Phuc rang the executioner in Sydney and in a three-minute call he told him they had been betrayed. In the next few weeks both American hitmen slipped out of Australia and flew to Vietnam.

After the arrests at Spencer Street Station, the Royal Hong Kong Police Force Organised Crime and Triad Bureau hit five homes and offices identified as connected with The Brotherhood through international bank records.

At one of the flats in Kowloon were two men. One was Nguyen Hoa Ngoc – the man who had received the Marlboro promotional cap and flew with one of the Bui brothers from the US on 20 April.

During the search they found the original fax message demanding $400,000 from Ha. They also found a novel called *Until Proven Guilty*. Written inside it were two telephone numbers. One was the Sydney motel where the Bui brothers stayed from 3 to 5 May and the other was the Los Angeles home of the hitmen's parents.

Fingerprints on the fax also matched those of the person who mailed 1.3kg of heroin to the Australian Capital Territory in April 1996.

On 7 June the body was found in the Noble Park drain and police knew they faced an international murder investigation. Senior Detective Steve Tragardh of the homicide squad had a contact in a tobacco company who was able to provide information on the US Marlboro promotional caps. This breakthrough took the investigation to Los Angeles.

Detectives were able to identify six people involved in the kidnapping – two from Melbourne, two from London working from Hong Kong and two from the United States.

The old mates' network proved effective. A Victorian police inspector rang a friend from the Hong Kong force and asked for help. An Australian Federal Police agent in California used personal contacts to get local detectives to help find one of the kidnappers. A Melbourne policeman rang a friend at New Scotland Yard and the Flying Squad began searching for Brother Phuc.

On 17 June, 1997, Officer Zbigniew Hojlo from the Oakland Police Department and Sergeant Frank Sierras from the Emeryville Police Department flew from San Francisco and then drove to the Long Beach City College, where a man called Bui Quang Chuong was studying history. They said they wanted to talk to him over local extortion and fraud crimes. The nervous Bui puffed on cigarettes during the interview. One friendly policeman leant over and told him that while the office was officially non-smoking he could drag away freely as long as he made sure he put them out. Just to make sure, the policeman added, could he spit on the lit end of each butt to make sure they were out? The suspect was happy to oblige.

The kidnapper was relieved he was not asked any questions about Australia and left believing he was in the clear.

What he didn't know was the police were carefully putting the three butts into a special exhibit container filled with a bag of dry ice, ready for Hojlo to fly it to Melbourne to be DNA tested.

The tests established that Bui was likely to have once worn the baseball cap found in the Glen Waverley driveway. While the evidence wasn't enough to extradite Bui from the US, it showed police they were on the right track.

The investigations finally identified the suspects in the US, Hong Kong, Vietnam, Australia and Britain.

ABOUT ninety minutes out of Hanoi, in the Ha Tay Province of Vietnam, the Ministry of Public Security has built the Provisional Detention Centre. The jail is so remote that many of the inmates – and most of the guards – have rarely seen a white face.

When Steve Tragardh of the Victorian homicide squad and federal agents Stewart Williams and Laurie Grey headed from the Australian Embassy through Hanoi's chaotic streets on their way to the jail they knew they would have only one chance to talk to the man who, they believed, had killed Le in Springvale.

The investigators were tied to a strict timetable. They could interview Bui Tai Huu, the executioner who had flown to Australia from California to kill, but only from 9.30 to midday and again from 2pm until 4pm. Midday to 2pm had been reserved for lunch with the prison chiefs, as the guest of one Colonel Nam. Tragardh had so many questions that he requested to skip lunch. He was told this would be an insult – no lunch, no interview.

They arrived at the sprawling, single-storey prison, were taken to a room and sat at a table. Bui was ushered in. There were no shackles or handcuffs. There was no need. There was nowhere to run. Bui seemed relaxed, despite being interviewed for a murder that would earn him a hefty jail term in Australia. He refused to make admissions on tape but chatted amicably with Tragardh 'off the record.'

Before they were well into the story guards stopped the interview. It was time for lunch with the Colonel.

It was a banquet of pond fish, dogmeat, rice and jail-made brandy. Colonel Nam sat between Tragardh, whom he nicknamed 'The Strong One' and Williams, 'The Handsome One'. He grabbed at the blond hairs on Tragardh's arms and head, saying he had not seen a fair-haired person before.

He told the Australians that all the food and brandy had been prepared by inmates. Tragardh told him that wouldn't happen in Australia for fear that the prisoners would adulterate the food. Nam smiled when the statement was translated to him. He then explained it was not a problem here because if a prisoner tried that … the remainder of the explanation did not need to be translated, as the prison chief slowly ran his finger over his throat.

After lunch Tragardh was able to share a beer with Bui. Then he played his best card. The executioner was in jail because he had been arrested with a kilogram of heroin in Vietnam. If he stayed he faced certain execution, but if he gave evidence in Australia he would serve a sentence in Melbourne and leave jail alive.

But there was no deal. Bui said he wouldn't be going back to Australia with the visiting detectives. As Bui saw it he had no choice but to stay and be executed on the heroin charge. If he gave evidence about the syndicate in Australia it might save his life by keeping him in an Australian jail – but all his family in the United States would be murdered.

That was the power of Brother Phuc. According to the executioner, Truong could order an innocent family in America to be slaughtered from his jail cell in Melbourne, and would do it without hesitation. For the man who had executed other people himself, it was a case of 'if you live by the sword, you die by the sword.'

WHEN Brother Phuc was finally escorted onto the British Airways 747 at Heathrow by Extradition Squad detectives from New Scotland Yard, few on the packed flight knew he was a murder suspect heading to Melbourne for a Supreme Court trial.

Truong was brought in before any other passengers were allowed on the flight. He was handcuffed to Steve Tragardh and they sat in the last row of three seats in economy. Their handcuffed hands were hidden discreetly under a jumper.

The prisoner was wedged in the window seat, next to him was Tragardh and in the aisle seat was the head of the homicide squad, Detective Chief Inspector Rod Collins.

For security reasons, the two detectives and the suspect were allocated their own toilet, which remained locked. The reason was simple. Police feared another passenger could plant a weapon in the toilet for Truong to grab.

Tragardh told the man that he had hunted around the world they could all relax and enjoy the flight if he understood that he no longer gave the orders. On this trip he had to remember at all times that he was a prisoner and not a passenger.

Truong nodded in agreement. He had one request. 'Please, could you put a handkerchief under the handcuffs?' The Victorian policeman asked why. The prisoner indicated he was concerned the chunky metal cuffs could scratch his gold watch. It was a Gucci, worth more than a month's pay for a policeman. During the flight the handcuffs were removed and the suspect was allowed to scan the menu.

A flight attendant asked if he wanted a drink. He automatically answered, 'red wine', the habit of dozens of first class trips.

Tragardh reminded him that this was not a pleasure flight. He settled for Coca Cola. If Brother Phuc was worried about the court battle ahead it didn't affect his appetite. He ate Moroccan chicken, Italian salad, a cheese and tomato omelette, stir fried chicken with black bean sauce, pickled vegetables and a chocolate dessert.

After one meal he lent over to Tragardh and said with a smile, 'Better than prison food.' Which, of course, is a matter of opinion.

Truong later said that he had difficulty understanding English. The problem was so great that the courts would later order that transcripts of the committal evidence should be translated to Vietnamese at a cost of $60,000.

But his language problems did not seem to worry him on the flight. He managed to kill time on the plane listening to the comedy channel – in English. And he laughed at the right places.

BROTHER Phuc was sentenced to an effective twenty-five years in jail for kidnapping and murder by Justice Frank 'The Tank' Vincent in the Melbourne Supreme Court. For the sentencing, all visitors to the court were searched and checked with metal detectors because of fears of a plot to free Truong. He stood in the dock as Justice Vincent's remarks were translated to him. At the end the accused, neatly dressed in a blue shirt and pressed slacks, bowed to the judge and his legal team. He then turned to the body of a court and began passing instructions to a group of Asian men and women.

He put his hand to his mouth in a gesture to his supporters that they should immediately start making phone calls. He was now a prisoner, but he still called the shots.

POSTSCRIPT: Mrs Ha is a devout Buddhist. She has decided to move to Melbourne because she wants to be near the spirit of her son.

Tough Silk

The prosecution case, already weak, was terminally damaged when the woman who made the complaints against Lovitt was arrested a few months later.

COLIN Lovitt, Queen's Counsel and murder defence expert, was sitting in a North Melbourne bar nursing a fresh beer and an old hangover when his mobile phone rang. It was a newspaper reporter asking if he wished to comment on his pending arrest on rape charges.

The journalist told him a woman had complained to police that only hours earlier she had been assaulted by the respected lawyer in his Carlton apartment.

Stunned, he refused to comment and put the phone down. Within a minute it rang again – this time it was a reporter from *The Age* with the same story. The expensive QC gave the journalist some free legal advice to be careful about what he wrote before ending the conversation.

He went home – 'I was devastated' – but around midnight went to *The Age* office to pick up a paper to see if there was a story that he was under investigation.

There wasn't.

But having been the defence barrister in more than 130 murder cases and observed headline-hungry media packs scavenging for salacious quotes he knew this story wasn't going to disappear. He didn't have to wait long. Just after 7am next day the 3AW Rumour File ran a story that a prominent barrister had been charged with rape. By 8am every television and radio station had caught up, and were ringing him to ask for interviews. 'I felt like a prisoner in my own home,' he said.

It was just the start of a ten-month battle that ended with five criminal charges being quietly withdrawn by the Office of Public Prosecutions on the grounds of 'public interest.'

Lovitt, Victoria's best known defence barrister, remains angry and bitter about the experience, believing his public humiliation was at least partially motivated by some he has offended during his thirty-year legal career.

But how did one of the toughest, most streetsmart lawyers in the trade end up being charged with a string of tawdry offences – and why were they discarded without any public examination?

TO some people lunch is a meal, to others it is an event. To Colin Lovitt, fifty four, it can be a marathon. President of the Carlton Cricket Club, vice-president of the Carlton Social Club, Convenor and former President of the Criminal Bar Association and long-time member of the Melbourne Press Club, he is a man who loves company, conversation and liquid refreshment.

Sunday, 28 March, 1999, was to be a big day, even by Lovitt's standards. It was to be the annual 'Endless Lunch' at the up-market Matteo's Restaurant in Brunswick Street, Fitzroy. It began around 1pm and for the hardy would finish thirteen hours later.

There were top quality wines and food, a band, opera singers, aerobics sessions and a light-hearted debate on whether smoking should be banned in restaurants. Lovitt and business-man John Elliott spoke for the smokers while Sam Newman and a police inspector spoke for the health conscious. More than seventy people went to the lunch and most drifted away by the evening, but a small, hard core ploughed on.

Among them was a woman in her late twenties whom Lovitt had met at the lunch the previous year. According to the barrister, he was sitting with about seven people 'relieved' the event he had helped organise had gone so well. Not wanting a good night to end he 'made the mistake of inviting everyone back to my place.' Only one accepted. The young woman.

'I had only met her twice before, was not remotely interested in her romantically and I knew she was not interested in me. But try telling that to those who want to put their own gloss on events,' he was to say later.

What happened then will never be tested in open court but what can be established is that during the dispute and the protracted aftermath there was no evidence of rape or gross sexual misconduct.

Lovitt says the woman became abusive, threw compact discs at him, dropped a wine glass over the balcony and then slept on the bed while he dozed on the couch. She then left in a rage around 7.30am. He says she returned, banged on the door, entered the apartment in search of her jacket and became abusive again.

He said he believed she was 'out of control and was going to assault me again or smash something else so I tackled her and sat on her ribs. I pinned her in an attempt to render her harmless.' He said he weighed 'twice as much and towered over her' and 'she rapidly calmed down' after he restrained her.

She left the apartment but later went to the Carlton police station to make a complaint that she had been attacked.

She had old bruising on her face from an accident and an unexplained red mark on her face.

While she was in the police station Lovitt was at another

183

lunch, unaware he was now the subject on an intense police investigation. His barrister, Con Heliotis, QC, later described it as 'akin to a murder investigation.'

Lovitt believes some police tipped off the media, even before the woman has signed her statement. By 5.30 that evening the press were after him for a comment.

'I haven't the slightest doubt that some police took an unholy delight in contacting the media to maximise my embarrassment.'

A week later a warrant was served to let police search his apartment. They took his robe, the doona, fluff from the carpet, a pair of shorts, a CD and a broken CD cover. They had already photographed and collected the broken wine glass in the lane six floors below. None of the exhibits assisted the investigation.

The man who has rigorously cross-examined police hundreds of times about search procedures watched as police examined his possessions. 'It is a very different feeling when it happens to you.'

Meanwhile, he was to feel the brunt of the rumours that swept the Bar. He heard colleagues claim he had broken a woman's nose and jaw and was about to be charged with rape.

'The Bar is a cesspit when it comes to gossip. There are quite a few counsel who are like a pack of vultures dying to think the worst. They chortle away at other people's expense.'

Barristers who every day solemnly lecture juries on the importance of the presumption of innocence gleefully condemned Lovitt as guilty and enjoyed seeing their high-profile colleague squirm.

For the first time in twenty-nine years the outgoing barrister felt uncomfortable going to his office at Owen Dixon Chambers and felt vulnerable – not to strangers – but to legal identities he had known for years who wanted to believe unproven allegations.

'I received many messages of support from many decent people,' he said, but added that he remains 'somewhat disenchanted' with the Bar.

THERE is no doubt that many police and some fellow barristers enjoyed watching the confident Lovitt cut down publicly during the months he stood accused. He has the ability to offend and enrage – in and out of the courtroom.

He is known as one of the toughest cross-examiners in the business and some take offence at his tactics. 'There are people who think I go in too hard but no-one can ever say that I have done anything dishonest,' he says with a voice timbred by decades of good reds and bad cigarettes.

He has taken on many high profile cases, including defending Greg Domaszewicz over the murder of Jaidyn Leskie, and was a constant critic of police methods at the Coroner's Court when representing the family of Graeme Jensen, a man shot dead by police in 1988.

In the long-running police shootings inquest he was particularly severe on John Hill, a respected homicide squad investigator. After one savage cross examination Lovitt saw Hill wandering through the car park of the Coroner's Court. 'I said to him, "Cheer up, it's really just a day in court, don't take it too seriously".'

Hill responded: 'It's all right for you – you haven't just seen your career go down the toilet.'

Detective Senior Sergeant Hill was later charged over his handling of the Jensen matter. Although the charges would certainly have been withdrawn, he committed suicide in September, 1993, days before he was to be cross examined in another case – again by Colin Lovitt.

Ironically, Lovitt made no secret of the fact he believed the charges brought against Hill and several other police over the Jensen death were ridiculous and expressed that view while giving evidence in court.

But some police never forgave Lovitt over the death of a colleague. Others held grudges over his take-no-prisoners attitude in court. Some prosecutors have no time for the barrister who has wounded them in heavy legal clashes. For the past twenty years he has attended the annual homicide squad party. Late last year he was confronted by one detective who made it clear he felt Lovitt was not welcome.

Yet, while there is no shortage of police who will bag the hard-nosed brief, there are others who see Lovitt as a great fighter who does the best for his client. 'He has tried to tear shreds off me in the (witness) box and when you leave the court almost punch drunk he'll walk over and say "let's have a beer". It is just business and he is good at his,' a veteran detective said.

At least one high-profile policeman and several judges were prepared to give character evidence for Lovitt if his trial had gone ahead.

Lovitt, the son of an *Age* photographer, toyed with the idea of being a journalist before turning to the law. While finishing university he was a secondary school maths teacher. 'I would have loved to have been a teacher if the wages were better.'

It is clear that Lovitt likes a lifestyle that doesn't come cheap but money is not his driving force – there is more money and less stress in corporate law or picking open loopholes in tax legislation for big business.

But, despite the way he has been treated, the 'Embarrister' defended a financially struggling man for nothing because a serious conviction would have cost the defendant his job.

The man was a policeman.

IT took police five months of investigation before they charged Lovitt with five offences. False imprisonment, intentionally causing injury, recklessly causing injury, common law assault and indecent assault.

As he was being informed by his solicitor, the tenacious Tony Hargreaves, that the charges had been served his mobile telephone rang. It was a *Herald Sun* reporter asking for a comment. Lovitt remains convinced that some police were feeding the media snippets as a pay back for old court battles.

He also maintains that some police ensured the charges were as extreme as possible. For example, he says, the indecent assault related to an allegation he tried to kiss the woman – a charge he vehemently denies – and the unlawful imprisonment related to pinning her to the floor after she returned voluntarily to the flat.

'They must have thought that all their Christmases had come at once and that this was a wonderful opportunity. They were ridiculous charges, designed to humiliate.'

Police sources say that expert investigators from the Rape Squad looked at the allegations within twenty-four hours of the complaint and concluded there wasn't sufficient evidence to prove any sexual offences.

They based their opinion on the fact that both parties were drunk, there was no independent corroboration, no strong forensic evidence and possible credibility problems as the complainant suffered from blackouts on the night.

The case went back to Carlton CIB where investigations continued. Finally, detectives handling the case recommended assault and unlawful imprisonment charges be laid, but the Detective Senior Sergeant supervising the case said the evidence was too weak to justify a prosecution.

The unlawful assault charge was laid because of Lovitt's admission that he pinned the woman down. 'What was I to do – allow her to attack me because she was a woman?' he asks.

It is believed that, ultimately, an acting Detective Inspector authorised laying the charges.

The matter was not referred to the Office of the Director Public Prosecutions for a legal opinion before Lovitt was charged. Police sources said the investigators originally did not recommend the indecent assault charge. It is not known when it was added it to the list.

Police launched an internal investigation into allegations that information from the complainant's statement was leaked to a prominent member of the Bar who was not connected to the defence or prosecution. The barrister denied seeing the document, but a senior member of the Rape Squad was later transferred.

There will be no independent examination of exactly what happened in Lovitt's apartment. But what can be established is that the prosecution case, already weak, was terminally damaged when the woman who made the complaints against Lovitt was arrested a few months later during an alcohol-related disturbance in which her behavior mirrored Lovitt's version of events in his apartment.

The case was formally withdrawn – the day the four-day Magistrates' Court hearing was to begin. A Sydney QC in to prosecute and the legal costs would have been around $100,000 if it had gone ahead.

In the eyes of the law Colin Lovitt is innocent. The charges have blown away – but the experienced counsel fears he could remain tainted.

For all his knowledge of detailed legal and Latin expressions he prefers to put it more succinctly. 'Shit sticks.'

CHAPTER 12

The Two-up King

*'Gawd, this must be some good game if
people are prepared to die for it.'*

ONCE, every taxi driver worth the fare knew where Nappy Ollington's floating two-up game was. No matter where the game surfaced after the latest police raid, within a day everyone in the know was in the know. On big nights Nappy would have to lock the doors, and the cash would pile up beside the ring as bet covered bet in the ancient game of chance that runs with deadly fairness: even money, heads against tails.

Nappy ran Melbourne's most famous two-up game for almost thirty years, but he had been spinning the pennies long before that, back to when he was a barefoot kid in the mean streets of South Melbourne in the Depression.

There were other two-up games around when he hit the big-time in the 1950s, but he became Melbourne's two-up king in the 1960s. Nappy loved the game and, for a long time, it repaid him well. He coined the saying that two-up players will play anywhere, as long as there's nowhere better — and, for a long time, he made sure there was nowhere better. The more players who passed his doorman's eagle eye, the more bets were laid, and the more winners there were to pay 'the shop' ten per cent.

Time was when Nappy lived in a big house in Middle Park. In those days he bought a new Ford Fairlane every other year and flew his teenage sons interstate to pick up the proceeds of Quadrella betting plunges on the races. He lived well and, when he was cashed up, so did those around him.

'They were great days,' he says reverently, like an old fighter reliving the glory of the long-ago night he won a title bout. Fighters and gamblers have something in common — they tend to keep going until they lose — and Nappy Ollington is both fighter and gambler. So it's not surprising the old champ still dreams of a comeback for the game he's loved all his life.

THESE days, there's hardly a taxi driver who'd know who Nappy Ollington is, let alone where to find him. He lives a quiet life with his second wife, Doreen, in an apartment in one of West St Kilda's old bayside buildings.

The old two-up king is now more than seventy but looks a decade younger. The boxer's biceps still swell under his tee-shirt, and he has the impatient tread of the all-round sportsman he used to be. His eyes are striking: blue-grey, like gun metal, and piercing under bushy dark brows and a full head of hair. For a man who is supposedly retired, he's bursting with energy and ideas. And stories. He can spin them as well as he used to spin the pair of century-old pennies he keeps in a drawer.

As colourful identities go, Nappy Ollington takes some tossing. If his life story were a film the script writer would be accused of going over the top. It reads like a collaboration between Damon Runyon, Frank Hardy and C.J. Dennis after a long and liquid lunch. But it's his story, and he's sticking to it.

Nappy is the classic cheeky battler who survived childhood on the wrong side of the tracks and had a crack at the high life. What he heard and saw along the way is a chapter of Melbourne's unwritten history, a tale that stretches back to the days of John Wren and Squizzy Taylor.

You had to be tough to get by, and he was. His parents made sure of that by giving him nothing much but a pair of names that would make a West Indian cricketer blush. Anyone called Lionel Vivian Ollington in working class Melbourne in the Depression was guaranteed two things: he'd learn to defend himself, and he'd get a nickname.

But why 'Nappy'? His explanation is that he was a happy little boy whose disposition reminded a neighbour of a popular Aboriginal everyone in the neighbourhood called Nappy. But Ollington's good humour didn't extend to people poking fun at him. A natural athlete with fast hands, he wasn't just a tough proposition in a street fight. As a youngster he beat a string of pro boxers in the ring at Festival Hall until his grandmother made him promise to hang up the gloves.

He worked on the waterfront as a young man. Shovelling coal in and out of the holds of ships made him strong, and he ran every day to overcome the painful rheumatic joints that plagued him as a teenager. He overcame it so well that he won the Wharfies' Gift foot race at the annual Wharfies' Picnic, running barefoot. He never touched alcohol and it gave him an edge.

He played League football for Footscray in 1953, the year before the club won the flag, but is just as proud of starring in three local football premiership sides in one week — a record he reckons only the late, great Ted Whitten equalled. Not bad for a little bloke ('nine stone, dripping wet') who carried a lot of injuries. But that's all just incidental stuff, really. What he wants to be remembered for is the part he played in the game he loves even more than football.

It's more than sixty years ago, but he still remembers the moment that two-up hooked him.

FLASHBACK to South Melbourne, late 1930s. There was a regular two-up game outside the Golden Fleece Hotel. Nappy and his brother Billy were usually hungry, and the drinkers and punters would often shout them a sausage roll or a pie.

The boys were mesmerised by the money tossed down by the gambling men. Kids who never handled more than copper coins could hardly believe it when they saw a 'ten-bob' note thrown in the ring by some hardened gambler.

One evening the police raided the game. 'Everybody ran,' he laughs, reliving the scene. 'A bloke called George Bryce was running the game. He ran off down Montague Street — and kept going even when the police fired two shots after him. I thought to myself: "Gawd, this must be some good game if people are prepared to die for it".'

Gambling attracted young Ollington, like others in that time and place, because he had little to lose. The family had landed in Port Melbourne from Smithton in Tasmania when he was seven, in about 1934. The only thing his parents had plenty of was children. Nappy was youngest of five.

His father, an axeman, went to Gippsland in search of timber work and rarely returned; their mother did the best she could in the slums of South Melbourne.

His three older sisters left home as soon as they could, his mother took up with a man he hated, and he and his brother mostly fended for themselves, apart from their grandmother's help. Memories of his mother are jarring. 'She was a cruel woman. She had this little red whip and chased us with it, on her bike. Other times she would make us chew dry epsom salts or take castor oil as punishment. It was barbaric.'

He and his brother were often reduced to begging for food, but he always hoped for something better. 'Nobody had nothing, but nothing was plenty for us,' he says cheerfully.

When war broke out in 1939, jobs were plentiful. He left school after seventh grade and started at the Kraft factory, nailing the tops on wooden crates. One day he ran into a favorite teacher. 'He asked what I was doing and I told him, working at the cheese factory. He said I was one boy who should have gone to university.'

Which, in a way, Nappy did, though not the one the kindly teacher meant. Young Ollington had no chance of going to a bricks-and-mortar university to be lectured and tutored into a profession. All he had, apart from a few shillings a week in wages, was a head for figures, plenty of nerve and a reputation for defending himself on and off the football field, where he was the local champion.

It gave him early entry to a different university ... running his own little two-up game as a teenager. Sometimes it was on the footpath outside the local pubs. On Sunday mornings, the needy and the greedy would gather in the park near the Rising Sun hotel until the local policemen broke up the game.

It was an education that made him a keen student of human nature, the mathematical laws of chance, the criminal law governing gambling, and the primitive law of the jungle. He was just sixteen the first time someone tried to stand over him for his money. It was his first examination, and he passed.

As the aggressor moved towards him, Ollington glanced down and said: 'Wait until I take off me watch.' He chuckles at the memory. 'The silly boy, he did. And he went to sleep.' In the split-second that the would-be standover man hesitated, it was over. Nappy got in first and won the takeover battle by knockout.

His reputation grew. By the time the war was over he was eighteen and ambitious. There were three big two-up games in Melbourne at the time: 'Chungy's' in Prahran, 'Daley's' in Carlton and 'The Sniper's' in North Melbourne and Footscray. The Prahran game was closest to South Melbourne, and Nappy knew a boxer called Young Jocka who helped 'mind' the game.

'They liked strong people working for them, so I went there,' he says casually of his first venture into the bigtime. 'After a couple of years Charlie Daley split with his partner over at Carlton. He asked me to form some sort of partnership between him and another bloke called "Tommy". He said we would put in 200 pounds each, equal shares.'

He scraped up the money and became a partner in the game, based in a room behind a nightclub opposite Queen Victoria market. Ollington later found out neither of his partners had actually put up their share of the money. Now, he relishes the joke against himself. 'Here I am sweeping up every night while they count the take — and I'm the only one who put in my share. I'm supposed to be the strong bloke, and I'm the patsy!'

The police gaming branch ran occasional raids on two-up schools, more as a gesture than as a real attempt to stamp them out. The only way to stop them would be to raid them every week and, in those days, neither State Government nor police wanted to waste time doing that. But the police command took a prudent interest in who was connected with the games.

In 1957, Nappy got his lucky break. His version is that while one of the partners, Charlie Daley, was in hospital, a senior figure in the police gaming branch called himself and 'Tommy' into his office for a meeting.

He recalls the interview this way. 'The policeman guy said: "Tommy, you are not the right character to be involved in the game but you, Ollington, you work on the waterfront and I haven't heard any bad reports about you".'

That's how Nappy Ollington got a green light to run his game, on the tacit understanding it had to be well run. It didn't mean he was protected from the letter of the law, just tolerated.

'By the time Charlie Daley came out of hospital and says "Where do I stand?" it was too late. I told him I knew he hadn't put his share of the money in, so he had no comeback. That was the end of Charlie's involvement.'

THE TWO-UP KING

The police still ran raids and Ollington had to pay the price of prosecution — another fine, another minor conviction, another frantic search for another empty warehouse, which he would paint out 'really smick', as he puts it. Laurie Bull, an artistic wharfy, painted a huge picture of the great racehorse *Peter Pan,* and it went wherever the game did, a signature touch.

Nappy's game flourished. First he got 'the overflow' from the two other games on busy nights, then his game started to grow. The other proprietors weren't happy, as he found out when two notorious heavies, Harold Nugent and Joey Turner, visited one day, but not to play.

'They said I was starting to be a bit of a nuisance. So I got my cousin Kevin Watterson to come down. Kevin was the boxing trainer, trained Rocky Mattioli later, and a better bloke never trod shoeleather. He was a handsome man, Kevin, but he was frightened of no-one. They threatened him with a bomb through his window and he said just said to them: "Don't miss".'

The showdown never came because, he says, a mutual acquaintance got out of jail around that time and had a word to Nugent and Turner 'and the pressure was taken off.'

'So now Nappy's flying,' he says, leaning forward on his couch. 'To run a top game at that time you had to be a psychologist. You had to handle the police and you had to handle these parasites.' By 'parasites' he means standover men.

There were a few of them over the years. 'Even before Charlie Daley got out of hospital I was approached by a bloke called "Frogmouth" and one called Johnny Johansen, who wanted to be sort of partners in the game. But they weren't cut out for two-up. Johansen frightened the clients and, in the end, I told them it was no good. They weren't partners any more. One Sunday morning Johansen comes running into the game, roaring like a big gorilla, scaring people. So I send for Kevin, my cousin, and he has words with Johansen. I put Kevin in as my partner after that.

'One night afterwards I get pulled out of the game to say there's someone outside who wants to see me. There's a car in a lane off Cobden Street. A guy in the passenger seat has a rifle levelled at me. I didn't know him but I knew the one in the driver's seat. I'm terrified of guns, but I said to them "We'll see who's going to win" and walked away, expecting to be shot in the back.

'Later, we moved the game to Brunswick Street in Fitzroy. One night I'd been at the fights and when I got back there'd been trouble at the game. Johansen had arrived with a bloke called Johnny Morrison, who'd king hit Kevin and broken his nose, but that didn't stop Kevin and he soon got on top of him. When I saw Kevin was hurt, I was livid.

'Johansen was big, but God's fair — he gives big men big hearts and little men bigger hearts. A pool cue fell on the floor and I knew Johansen would try to get it. But one of my staff was quick and alert, he stood on it so Johansen couldn't pick it up. I put together probably the best two punches of my life. He fell so hard he broke his leg. I never saw either of them again after that.

'The thing is, if you can't defend your game and your clients, you might as well close down.'

Police raids were annoying, but didn't affect business in the early days. Ollington's funniest memories are of the times he persuaded every player booked in a raid to insist on being taken to the watchhouse, because he knew the police hated doing paperwork for sixty people who would be released within hours. As soon as they got inside the holding cell at the watchhouse out would come a 'kip' and pennies and the game would resume.

The game attracted what he calls a 'cross section'. Even now, he won't reveal the well-known people who dropped in to spin the pennies or to bet on the side. But the regular crowd included footballers, jockeys, trammies, taxi drivers, and detectives who came to see who was cashed up, and stayed to play. When the American heavyweight boxer Jimmy Ellis came to Melbourne to fight Joe Frazier in 1975 he dropped into the game and threw heads three times running. (Legend has it Ellis also attended a party run by a well-known socialite who persuaded him to break the boxer's cardinal rule of abstaining from pleasures of the flesh before a fight, but that is another story.)

Regular players had nicknames. There was Scratchy Stan, Pizza Mick, Footscray Bill, Taxi Tom, and Eric The Red, a Steptoe-lookalike who spent his days busking with a mouth organ in the city so that he could play two-up at night. Losers were shouted a taxi fare home. Winners paid their ten per cent premium to 'the shop' after three winning bets. Nappy paid for the funerals of several of his regulars. 'My grandmother once told me it was better to give than receive,' he says.

'We ran the game strictly. We wouldn't allow any alcohol, and made sure there was never any trouble. No loutish behavior.'

After the TAB started operations in the 1960s the game that diggers had played in two world wars was a casualty of the State's push to monopolise gambling profits.

The police raids intensified. The other big games closed, which concentrated police pressure on Nappy's. He had to move more often, playing an exhausting game of hide and seek. One night, he says, at the time of the Commonwealth Heads of Government Meeting in Melbourne in 1981, a partner was running the game for the night when word reached Ollington at home that a raid was on. He arrived in time to see armed police in boiler suits and jack boots with police dogs, as if they were confronting terrorists. It seemed to him a heavy-handed way to treat the national game old soldiers play every Anzac Day.

By 1984 Ollington was a grandfather in his fifties. With his sons, Steven and Robbie, he was looking at ways of exporting the game he believed legalised gambling had ruined.

The family was keen to concentrate on joint ventures in the United States and elsewhere, modifying the game to suit casinos.

At home, meanwhile, 'I could smell change, and I didn't like it,' says Nappy. Police pressure had driven two-up so far underground that few legitimate people wanted to play. By criminalising it, the authorities had ensured only criminals risked playing.

He sold his interest in the game, and it moved a step closer to extinction. He reckons he got a rough spin from the authorities and the big end of town. For twenty-five years the standover men didn't put him off his game but, in the end, the men in suits did. As he sees it, politicians and bureaucrats protected the long-term business interests of the Government and its favoured operators to set up other forms of gambling.

Nappy shakes his head sadly, and says that casinos have choked the life out of the great Australian game. If two-up had been set up properly in casinos it would now be a genuine tourist attraction — unlike the homogenised standard gambling games played in every casino in the world.

'The police brought representatives of the Wrest Point casino to sit in on my game for a week to get the feel of how to run the game — and they learnt nothing. The casinos have destroyed the best game in the world. They took it and created Bay Thirteen, with drunks screaming and singing so no-one can hear and get a bet on. That's not the way to run our national game.'

But he hasn't given up hope. The Ollingtons have proprietary games approved and operating overseas and have developed a new casino version of the traditional game that Nappy firmly believes will be Australia's greatest gaming attraction, and a huge money spinner. 'Bigger than the atom bomb' is the way he puts it. But that's not really what motivates a grandfather in his seventies.

It's more a matter of pride. If it all works out and the Ollingtons make a comeback with legal two-up, he reckons someone might just make a film about his life and times.

They could call it *Don't Get Mad, Get Evens*.

CHAPTER 13

No More Cops and Robbers

*A group of criminals began to believe
that some detectives in the squad were just
as keen to kill a crook as catch one.*

RAY WATSON had been a policeman for just eight hours when he had his first run-in with higher-ranking colleagues.

He had been out to celebrate his graduation and was driving down the Maroondah Highway on Melbourne's eastern outskirts well over the limits, both in speed and alcohol.

He was driving a friend's white E Type Jaguar, in his own words, 'at speed', when he saw a blue flicker in the rear view mirror grow into an ominous flashing light.

Two stern-faced policemen hopped from a divisional van, but the newest copper in Victoria was unfazed. 'It's all right, boys,' he yelled, 'I'm in The Job.'

He well could have been out of it if the two police had not been quite so tolerant.

'They were very irate and told me in no uncertain terms that my behaviour was unacceptable,' Watson was to recall of that roadside encounter.

'It taught me a lesson about motor-vehicles and sobriety.'

Recruits to the Police Academy come from a wide range of backgrounds, but even then the lanky Watson stood out. He was the only known trainee who was a failed rock star – and 188 cm tall.

He had been the bass guitarist in a band – appropriately called The Fix. 'I started as a lead guitarist and devolved from there,' was the way he described a shortlived musical career.

Watson was a scholarship student at Strathmore High until he fell out with the principal. 'We decided that we should part company and as he was comfortable in his position we agreed that perhaps I would move on.'

Essendon Grammar was the next stop, although his attention was shifting from schoolwork to nightclubs.

He took to the road with the band but got the message that lucrative recording contracts, lubricious groupies and world tours were unlikely to be part of his future when the police at Pyramid Hill suggested the musicians move on, out of town. 'Everyone's a critic,' he says without rancour.

'They felt we were not the right type to be in their country oasis. It then began to dawn on me that my musical career was unlikely to blossom.'

The band broke up – 'artistic differences' – to pursue solo projects. Watson's first 'project' was a mutually unsatisfying stint in the public service. He didn't fancy the service and it didn't fancy him. Then, like many young people, he decided to travel.

But, characteristically, he chose his own path.

For three years, he wandered through South America, the West Indies and the US. It was during this period that he tasted the criminal justice system from different perspectives.

He was robbed in Jamaica, locked up in Argentina and worked as a store detective in San Francisco. He said he ended up in a South American jail for being 'a known smart-arse in a public place.' He was also to find there were internationally recognised police methods for dealing with young men with bad attitudes.

'They put me in a cage on the back of a Jeep, it was like an open divvy van, and they took me around the town, stopping and starting, to bounce me around a little.'

It worked. He returned to Australia in 1972 determined to be a policeman.

'I suppose I had a bit of a *Boy's Own* attitude to being a copper. I always wanted to be a detective and chase the bad guys.'

He graduated sixth out of twenty four in squad five of 1973. He breezed through the exams but received the most demerit points for rowdy and disruptive behaviour during the five-month course.

Watson's squad mate and now homicide crew leader, Detective Senior Sergeant Charlie Bezzina, said Watson has not changed.

'He was self-assured and prepared to speak his mind even back then. He was always prepared to laugh off any dramas that came his way. We looked up to him. What you saw was what you got with Ray.'

It was as well that Watson wanted to be a detective because at times he was to prove to be a menace when in uniform.

While still a trainee he was assigned to traffic duty at the corner of Russell and Exhibition Streets. Within minutes he had directed two cars into a collision and created a hopeless traffic jam.

'Five of my class mates were offering full support by falling over laughing. The instructor had to stand behind me, waving my arms around like I was a muppet.

'Senior police and myself were in full agreement; traffic was not for me.'

He was involved in various areas of policing, from Ascot Vale to Broadmeadows. In 1985 he was appointed the head of a taskforce set up to blitz Melbourne because of violent gang activity. 'We had a zero tolerance policy. Anyone seen committing a crime was arrested. The word spread as we knew it would and the results were outstanding. Even when they were thinking of committing a crime we would lock them up. We were very intuitive – it was a bit spooky how we could read their minds.'

But in 1986 the underworld was changing and there was a new violent edge between police and criminals. Watson, the wisecracking, guitar-playing detective, was to be caught up in it. He was to become a leading player in what was to be an undeclared war between a group of armed robbers and the squad paid to arrest them.

Watson was on leave when an armed robbery squad detective, Mark Wylie, was shot on Anzac Day, 1986, by one of the gang who had exploded a car bomb outside the Russell Street police building.

Watson was told he would be reporting for duty at the squad on Monday. 'I was happy with what I was doing but I was given no choice. But within two weeks I knew this was for me.'

He said the bandits they chased were professional armed robbers. 'They were violent and well researched. They were the big names of crime. In those days there were about three bank armed robberies a week compared with about three a month now.'

The armed robbery squad was conducting raids at least four times a week, always with guns drawn. A group of criminals began to believe that some detectives in the squad were just as keen to kill a crook as catch one.

The police were of the belief the bandits were prepared to shoot detectives to avoid arrest. As the tension built between the two armed groups the likelihood of killings increased.

NO MORE COPS AND ROBBERS

On Christmas Eve, 1986, Watson was driving home – and, like everyone, else he was looking forward to a break from guns and robberies. He was not to get one.

He was diverted to an armed robbery at the National Bank in South Melbourne. Eventually police were able to conclude that a group of criminals in the North Melbourne-Kensington area were responsible for a series of nine armed robberies.

Police hired a flat opposite one of the gang members and started to gather intelligence. They found that one of the crew – Mark Militano – was planning an armed robbery the next day.

Police expected that Militano would leave the block of flats and head home. The Special Operations Group was assigned to arrest him on March 25, 1987.

But Militano went the other way, in the direction of the armed robbery squad. Watson made a split-second decision to arrest the suspect. Militano was shot dead in the ensuing confrontation.

'If he had not raised his gun at me he would have been apprehended in the normal fashion. I shot at him before he shot at me,' Watson explained later.

He said the Coroner found that he had acted lawfully, but the taking of a human life weighed heavily on him.

'For the next year you have doubts. I was doing about one raid a week then and I had these thoughts. What if it happens again, will I put my colleagues at risk?'

That June a convicted armed robber, Frank Valastro, was shot dead by the Special Operations Group during a police search.

A group of criminals believed the armed robbery squad was out of control and trying to kill them. Police intelligence indicated the criminals planned to follow an armed robbery squad detective home and shoot him in his driveway.

Then the gang hatched a two for one plot. If the armed robbery squad killed another mate they would kill two police.

On October 11, 1988, members of the armed robbery squad shot a suspect, Graeme Jensen, when they went to arrest him at Narre Warren.

Thirteen hours later, two police, Steven Tynan and Damian Eyre, were shot dead in Walsh Street, South Yarra, in an alleged payback for the death of Jensen.

The deaths didn't stop. The armed robbery squad tried to catch suspects in the act so the evidence they would present in court would be beyond dispute. It didn't always go according to plan.

On July 28, 1992, police shot dead a bandit, Normie Lee, when he and others grabbed a million dollars at Melbourne Airport. The Special Operations Group was waiting and Lee was shot dead after threatening police with a gun.

The Coroner criticised the armed robbery squad in its planning for the arrest of Lee and the other two bandits – criticism that Watson still refuses to accept as valid.

'We believed there was only one way to handle it. People forget that it is the armed robbers who terrorise innocent people, who go armed to rob businesses. We just responded to the level of threat.'

In May, 1994, police shot dead another two bandits, Paul Skews and Stephen Crome, when they attempted to rob a real estate agent in Hampton Park. On the same day two guards and a man were shot during an armed payroll robbery at Chadstone.

'We didn't have a plan to eliminate criminals. We planned to eradicate the jackals who were preying on society by putting them in jail.

'There was never a conspiracy. After the Russell Street bombing we all knew we were vulnerable and we developed the attitude that it was not going to be us.'

Watson points out that the gangs of robbers who set up the big stick-ups in the 1980s and 1990s have all been convicted. These were the crews who often had inside information on security and payroll deliveries, who flew around the country to pull off massive armed robberies and planned their raids with military precision.

They had access to high-powered weapons and would sometimes franchise out jobs, providing plans, guns, disguises and even medical kits with antibiotics and pain killers for other criminal groups.

'Some of the main men were locked up and caught again years later, after their release, doing more jobs. I believe we destroyed an arm of the underworld. The armed robberies today are committed by junkies in the main, rather than by organised criminal groups.'

RAY WATSON was directly or indirectly connected in the death of four police and eight criminals. He lived on the edge, working in a squad that was always close to controversy.

Finally, senior police decided that Big Ray had gone too far and needed to be pulled up.

The order came down that Detective Senior Sergeant Ray Watson needed to be disciplined for a heinous internal crime.

He told a bad joke during a speech. Watson is an acknowledged master after dinner speaker, where his outgoing personality, sharp wit and great experience are seen to their full effect.

During the armed robbery squad's 25th anniversary celebrations on Friday, October 31, 1997, Watson was in full flight during his speech at the Hilton Hotel in front of 160 police and former squad members. He mentioned that at the time the Madame Tussaud's Exhibition and the internal police Ethical Standards Department were housed in the one complex.

'I went there the other day. I saw all these pale, lifeless dummies … then I went into Madame Tussaud's.'

It brought the house down and nearly took Watson's career

with it, there and then. While most of those in the room laughed, one table of senior officers remained poker-faced.

By the following Monday Watson was being dragged over the coals. He was forced to stand and apologise to all ethical standards police in their office and then was transferred to the missing persons bureau for six months.

'I enjoyed the experience of working at missing persons. Not necessarily the way I got there,' he reflects.

Watson didn't fit the stereotype of a typical armed robbery squad detective – he preferred Chardonnay to beer and living on his small country property to life in the suburbs. But even now he still wears the short-sleeved white shirts of a 1980s detective. The armed robbery squad motif of crossed guns tattooed on his right shoulder is visible through the thin shirt.

In an era when police who are colourful can be viewed with suspicion within their own organisation, Watson refused to change. At a time when police were discovering healthy lifestyles, Watson remained a heavy smoker.

As a concession to fitness he joined an informal armed robbery squad walking group – known as the 'Fat Boys Club' – whose members would power around Albert Park every day. It collapsed after some of the members insisted on stopping for a gasper half-way through the walk.

When the St Kilda Road crime department building was declared smoke free Watson's office remained suspiciously nicotine friendly. He would plead ignorance. 'We couldn't see the no smoking signs for the smoke,' he explained.

Strange things have happened in the armed robbery squad in Watson's time.

One of the detectives had become an expert in explosives in the army and used his skills in a series of dangerous practical jokes. He booby trapped other detectives' desks and seats, literally blowing them up. A reporter was once enjoying a drink in the armed robbery squad office – until he put out his cigarette in an ashtray filled with gunpowder.

The unfortunate reporter was set on fire in the small explosion and quick thinking detectives put him out with beer – 'and one glass of Chardonnay' adds Watson.

'Thank God he was surrounded by trained investigators who were able to save his life. He should have thanked us. We had often mused on the best way to extinguish a reporter who was on fire and beer was never considered the first option.'

The explosions stopped after the main perpetrator was blown up in a retaliation bombing that blew his desk to bits.

The squad was known for its hard-headed attitude but sometimes armed robbery squad detectives employed subtle tactics to get a confession.

In one case the suspect knew the evidence against him was compelling and he decided to make a deal with the investigators. He told them he was prepared to confess if they would do him a favour. He was going away for a long time so he asked if he could see his wife, for one best 'romantic' engagement.

The suspect and his wife were ushered into an interview room for some private time. After the meeting the man confessed and was later convicted.

When police were hunting the so-called 'Beanie Bandit', the veteran criminal Aubrey Broughill, the armed robbery squad believed he would turn up to his mother's funeral at Box Hill.

Surveillance police mingled with mourners, looking for the wanted man. One policeman, known as 'The Gnome', muttered into his concealed microphone that he had identified the suspect – wearing a dress.

Watson, sitting in a car with his team armed with shotguns, asked for confirmation of the old crook's apparently masterful disguise. Which was just as well, because when the trained observer had another look he realised the suspect actually was an elderly woman with a slight facial hair problem. In late 1999 the armed robbery squad was absorbed into the new armed offenders squad. After twenty-seven years in the force and a record fourteen years with the 'Robbers', Watson, at fifty, started to think of his future. 'The fuel that kept me going was genuine outrage for the victims, but after so many years and so many cases I felt it was beginning to diminish.'

The nature of policing was changing. There was more accountability and, for Ray Watson, less fun. 'The job has changed and for me the novelty had worn off. There is more emphasis on supervision and less on initiative.'

He could have moved into an administrative position but he was restless. 'I always said I would rather retire from the firsts than go back to the reserves.'

So it was that Ray Watson quit the 'Robbers', the CIB and the police force. He could have stayed a few more years to get a bigger superannuation cheque but argues that is not what it is about. 'I think when your enthusiasm starts to wane it is time to look for a new challenge.'

He has moved into private enterprise with a firm called Advent Security, where he will combine his great loves, public speaking and crime prevention – lecturing companies on how not to become armed robbery targets.

He gave a speech in a country town, in a district that had not suffered an armed robbery in years. He left to a standing ovation.

The local bank was robbed three days later.

As Ray was always the first to admit, nobody's perfect.

CHAPTER 14

Goldfinger

What sort of man runs a strip joint and
finds himself in this sort of mess?

RAYMOND Bertram Bartlett is a big man but, as that other Raymond (Chandler, that is) once wrote about another colorful character, he's 'no taller than a two-storey building and no wider than a beer truck.'

Raymond Bartlett's office matches the man himself. It covers most of the upstairs floor of a renovated warehouse and has enough room to park a beer truck. If it's not the biggest office in Melbourne, it runs a close second.

Here, surrounded by a bank of closed circuit television screens, a hidden tape recorder and an intercom, Bartlett is master of his chosen business.

That business is running the sort of place God-fearing people used to call 'a den of iniquity' and is vulgarly known as a strip joint: a place that stays open until dawn where men drink and pay young women to shed flimsy costumes and dance naked.

But that all happens below decks, where the money changes

hands. Up here, where it's counted, the office has been set up to look like someone's guess at how the library of a gentleman's club might be. Sort of.

The oval antique boardroom table is big enough for a Little League football team to play on, with a heavy soda siphon where the centre square would be.

The walls are lined with french-polished bookcases loaded with Encyclopedia and other heavy-duty examples of the bookbinder's craft, all in mint condition.

The desk is as big as the man behind it, its shiny surface as spotlessly tidy as everything else is in a place that would put some hospitals and most offices to shame. Some might say the business is sordid, but no-one can say it's grubby.

Bartlett is the proprietor of what is, after a recent court case, probably one of Australia's best-known tabletop dancing establishments. It is called Goldfingers and it's the sort of place where, you might think, illegal drugs would be easily obtained and often used, probably in conjunction with prostitution.

Not so, says Bartlett. The Olympics might have a drug problem but Melbourne's tabletop dancing venues do not, he insists. Nor do they condone any sexual contact on their premises. At least, his doesn't, and he's proud of it.

The fact is, there's a practical reason for such strictness, he says. If anyone is caught offering sex for sale or dealing in drugs Goldfingers stands to lose a licence to print money ... its liquor licence.

But, for the thousands of ordinary citizens who go past such places and wonder what goes on inside, it might come as a surprise to hear the big man's solemn opposition to drugs and sex for sale.

This is just one of the surprising things about the former truckie who has become, by default, the public face of what is formally known as the 'sexually explicit entertainment' industry in Melbourne. Another surprise is that he doesn't emerge as the violent 'pimp' figure many might have assumed he was after he was charged with assaulting one of his dancers. The case, which took more than two years to get to trial, ended in the county court in early 2000. He was fined $1000 – but had no conviction recorded against him.

For a man of his means, a $1000 fine seems little more than token punishment for a technical breach of the law. As he sees it, it's vindication: proof that a judge and jury believed his version of events above that of the dancer who made allegations against him after an ugly scene in his club in late 1997.

Monique Meenks, then nineteen, had just started work at the club, which is housed in an extension of the historic Kilkenny Hotel on the corner of King and Lonsdale Streets in the city.

The prim Edwardian surrounds of the Kilkenny's corner bar and dining room contrasts sharply with the dimly-lit luxury of Goldfingers, built in a converted store next door.

It was in here, shortly before midnight on 11 November, 1997, that there was a confrontation between the nightclub boss and the dancer that was to hit the headlines. About the only point both parties agree on is that Meenks had no idea that the 51-year-old man with the gold-rimmed glasses, the Falstaff figure and the cowboy boots, was her boss.

'He was just another dollar bill walking around the club,' she was to tell a court much later. Make that a fifty dollar bill, which was what Bartlett slipped her to dance for him – a deliberate overpayment, he was to say later, to test whether the new girl was breaking the rules by offering sexual favours, or trying to charge patrons more than the standard rate of ten dollars a song.

What happened next is still in dispute, although the jury made up its mind. Monique Meenks was to testify that Bartlett was drunk and that he groped her, then kicked her and spat on her. Bartlett was to deny this vehemently, insisting he had been forced to restrain the dancer by pinning her down when she had gone berserk, screaming and kicking him after he had accused her of trying to 'rip off' patrons, one of whom had complained earlier.

There was medical evidence – the dancer had bruises behind the knees and had sore ribs – injuries in keeping with Mr Bartlett's version of events, the court was to hear later.

After being removed from the club and put in a taxi by security staff, the dancer went to the police. Her injuries were not serious enough for police to send her to a police surgeon for assessment. Instead, she went to a private doctor, who confirmed the sore ribs and bruises. The injuries did not prevent her dancing next night – and ever since – at the nearby Men's Gallery, Goldfingers' closest competition.

Police didn't interview Raymond Bartlett until a fortnight later. In that interview, taped and later played in court, he stated firmly that he didn't need a lawyer, he answered every question in detail and he never wavered from his story. And the jury of six women and six men, mostly middle-aged, appeared to agree largely with the defence portrayal of Meenks as an opportunist out for a cash settlement.

Which, of course, poses a parallel question: what sort of a man runs a strip joint and finds himself in this sort of mess? An opportunist out for cash, a cynic might say.

In the 1960s James Bond film, Goldfinger is a stock villain in the Teutonic mould – all buttoned-up menace, fake accent and Nazi war criminal overtones, worthy inspiration for an Austin Powers satire. Raymond Bartlett is also a creature of the 1960s, but Goldfinger he isn't, bar a larger-than-life aura that comes with being a self-made millionaire whose belt buckle comes in the door a couple of seconds before he does.

The blue singlet was long ago replaced by the (open-necked) business shirt, but there's still a lot of truck in the man whose 'university' was driving interstate rigs. And he can talk like the insurance salesman he was until he took on the hotel game.

The language is salty, the accent as broad as his shoulders, there's a tattoo on his bicep and a temptation to say the two heavy gold rings he wears would pack a punch in a truckstop blue. But he's more businessman than bruiser – always was. It's true he left Prahran Tech at fourteen years old, but his father owned a bolt factory in Richmond and the young Bartlett grew up in the relative comfort of Armadale. But it didn't stop him wanting to drive trucks.

Much to his father's disgust, he worked in a service station and a factory for a while, then went to Adelaide when he turned sixteen so he could get a driver's licence two years early.

He got the licence, then a job delivering cakes in a truck. At eighteen, he returned to Melbourne, inherited enough from his grandmother to buy a car, then sold it and bought his own truck – 'an old International 180 semi-trailer' – for five thousand dollars.

It was 1966. The truck was slow and Bartlett had never driven beyond the tram tracks. He went to a transport depot in Footscray and lied about his interstate driving experience. He got the job – and took twenty-four hours to drive to Sydney.

'I was so tired I had a sleep at Seymour, the truck was so slow it would go backwards as soon as it saw a hill, and I was so nervous I stopped before I went down them. At Wodonga, I stopped at the Caltex roadhouse and asked how far Sydney was, and the waitress laughed and said I was only half way.'

After fifteen years at the wheel, he owned three trucks and employed two drivers, but he was no transport tycoon. Even then, he says, he hated drugs – refusing to take the 'pep pills' that others did to handle the endless hours on the road.

But he was articulate, and a shrewd negotiator. He became president of the Australian Transport Association and was a key figure – with the colorful Ted 'Greendog' Stevens – in setting up an interstate truck blockade in April 1979 to protest against the road tax that crippled owner-drivers.

The blockade took Bartlett on a week of living dangerously during which he flew from highway blockades to Parliament House by helicopter to negotiate a settlement with the then Premier, Rupert Hamer.

In one tense scene, he stood beside then Transport Minister, Rob Maclellan, in a Dynon Road truck depot and stared down a threat by angry fruit and vegetable market identities to blow up the place with high explosive if the trucks didn't roll. 'Maclellan's not a bad bloke,' he says warmly of a most unlikely ally, the refined Melbourne Grammar old boy and longtime Liberal politician.

As he reminisces, the big man slides a scrapbook across the desk. In it is every press clipping – and the original letter of agreement drafted and signed by the exasperated Premier after eight hours of argument.

The blockade was lifted, and road tax was repealed in every state. Soon after, Raymond Bartlett switched from driving trucks to insuring them, and got rich.

Along the way, in the early 1980s, he took a share in a Gold Coast nightclub and restaurant called Eliza's. It was the start of his involvement with hotels. He borrowed $2 million to take over the Toorak Hotel – the famous 'Tok H' – in 1985, and borrowed twice that for the Sentimental Bloke hotel in Bulleen. He also took over Silvers nightclub in Toorak, then the Hampton Hotel.

What he doesn't add, but others do, is that while at the Tok

H, he donated use of the hotel to the police for a day to raise money for the families of Damien Eyre and Steve Tynan, the two young constables murdered in Walsh Street, South Yarra. Around three thousand police arrived and raised $53,000.

He sold all his hotel interests in 1991, and took a year off before taking over a big hotel in Dandenong for four years.

'It was like running a war zone,' he grimaces, and it made him want a quiet, respectable city hotel for a change. Enter the Kilkenny, which in late 1996 had been empty for months.

In theory, it would be a classy late-night venue for Crown Casino staff after they finished work. In practice, King Street's nightclub image meant a conventional pub wouldn't work. After losing money for months, the new publican on the block knew he had to compete with the Men's Gallery and Bar 20 with strippers, or go out of business. Sex sells.

He enlisted Annette White, who runs the Miss Nude Australia contest, to organise the entertainment. Ms White and Helen Farrell, the club's general manager, recruited the dancers, and still handle the day-to-day running of the club. No men are involved in recruiting or managing the 'girls', he says.

'Any chick with half a brain can make it into a good business,' he enthuses.

'Of course, you get your scallywags, hence the vetting procedures. We don't want junkies. We don't want young kids just walking in off the street saying they want to be strippers. They've got to be eighteen, and we want contact numbers for next of kin to check that their parents know what they're doing. We do proper ID checks and we ask about drugs, and if they are professional dancers we get a reference from other clubs.

'The general public would assume we're exploiting the girls. The truth is we're their accountants, drug counsellors and their psychologists. 'Middle-class Australia would have no idea how it really is ... it could be their own daughters working here. There are five thousand dancers in Australia and thousands around the world.

'Most of them (Melbourne dancers) live in South Yarra, not shit suburbs, and they live well. I've got one here who's training to be a doctor, and another that speaks five languages. There's some brainy sheilas here.'

As he talks, the first shift of dancers files past the open office door from their dressing room – in their case, the undressing room – where they change from street clothes into very little. They wave and smile brightly and chorus 'Hi Ray' as they descend to where money waits to be made below.

Providing, of course, they stick to the ground rules for sanitising a dirty business: no touching by patrons, nothing closer than thirty centimetres to face or groin, one foot to be touching the floor at all times.

One young woman, wearing bleached blonde hair and a zebra-striped outfit, wiggles into the office pointing to a picture spread in a women's magazine and chirping 'I'm famous.'

She's nineteen, looks younger, and is excited about the publicity, though not about the magazine's statement that she earns $2000 a week. 'I just said some dancers can make up to that much,' she pouts.

The image the club wants, Bartlett says earnestly, is the 'girl next door'. Upmarket, he says, not sleazy. 'No sex,' he says firmly. 'We don't want to step on the brothel toes. You've got the (brothels) Top of the Town, and the Boardroom – they're all there.' The message is that the brothels don't serve alcohol, and Goldfingers and other tabletop venues don't serve sex.

That way, everyone gets a fair share of the sex industry dollar. It's called orderly marketing.

There's a risk, he concedes, that if strippers are desperate for more money than they get from dancing, they might be tempted to offer sex. It doesn't take a rocket scientist to calculate that the main motive for wanting extra money would be a drug habit.

That's why the clubs don't like hiring drug users, and why dancers with bruises from injecting themselves are 'counselled'. As in, if you're bruised, you don't work.

He produces another exhibit from his files: a heartwarming before and after picture story of a pretty teenager whom the good folks at Goldfingers helped kick heroin addiction.

Time for delicate questions. What about the underworld?

Bartlett talks about the 'Melbourne Safe City Accord', a committee chaired by a senior policeman to hose down potential trouble spots. The bottom line, he says, is that Melbourne's different.

Try to open a strip club in Brisbane and you'd get your legs shot off, he says. Sydney – you wouldn't even try because it's sewn up. In Perth, they'd kill you. Adelaide? Touch and go. Only in Melbourne is the 'industry' controlled so well, he says. No sir, there's no crooks in tabletop dancing here.

On the computer screen next to him the screen-saver flickers past. It is not, as one might imagine, soft porn images of the sort being enacted in the flesh below. The pictures on the screen are of athletic young women, but they are tennis players, with their clothes on. No doubt it makes a change from work.

One more question. Did the assault charges affect you?

'Look,' he sighs, 'that case cost the taxpayers probably $100,000 when it should have been solved in five minutes. I reckon it was only taken to court because it was me, because it was the sex industry. Now I go to joints and people who don't know me say: 'Aw, be careful of him, or he'll have you offed.'

It's fantasy. If I was such a big, bad crim what do you reckon would have happened to that Monique?'

One effect, he says, is that he's now wary of being set up. He points to the closed circuit video monitors and opens a cupboard door to reveal sophisticated tape-recording gear.

And the club? Did the court case keep people away? 'Nah,' he grins, 'the takings went up the week I was charged. Good publicity.'

CHAPTER 15

Lady's Day

It is a peaceful scene but the Magills are not at peace.
They are at a Melbourne cemetery and the daughter
they have come to visit is dead — murdered
by two men who have never been found

JOHN and Helen Magill packed the boot of the family car with two fold-up chairs, a portable wooden table, a thermos and a some fresh Christmas lilies picked that day from their neat suburban garden. They were off to see their youngest daughter. It was her birthday.

John didn't look at a map. Every week they travelled the same way, in the 1982 white Ford Fairlane that had taken their girl to church on her wedding day fourteen years earlier.

It was a beautiful autumn day for a birthday picnic – cloudless, sunny and almost still. They parked and set up their picnic gear on the manicured grass in the shade of a tall claret ash.

They sat, listening to the wrens that had been missing in recent visits, and could hear the rustle of the leaves directly above them. They could have been in the middle of the country but for the noise of a lone motor mower in the middle distance.

It is a peaceful scene but the Magills are not at peace. They are at a Melbourne cemetery and the daughter they have come to visit is dead – murdered by two men who have never been found. Their daughter is, or was, Jane Thurgood-Dove. She was shot dead in the driveway of her Niddrie home in front of her three children on Oaks Day, 1997.

In racing, they call it Ladies' Day, when thousands of women turn out in their finest clothes to see the best thoroughbred fillies in the land battle for supremacy at Flemington. But for the Magills, it will always be Lady's Day. Their sweet Jane's day, the saddest one on their calendar.

They sit, as they always do, next to the bronze memorial plaque in the Garden of Eternal Memories and ask why.

THURSDAY, 6 NOVEMBER, 1997* (OAKS DAY): It would have to be the worst day in the life of this family. Around 3.45 in the afternoon I was watering the back garden and as I often do at that time, thinking of Jane picking the children up from school to bring home. Jane was a very caring mother, the mum who stayed home and took care of the kids and the house.

Being Thursday and pay day they would wait for Mark to come home from work and then as a family would do the weekly shopping at the supermarket and get fish and chips on the way home. They all looked forward to that.

Helen and I ate an early dinner and around 5.45pm there was a knock at the front door. There were two men in dark suits who identified themselves as homicide detectives.

The police asked to come into the house as they had some bad news to tell us. Sitting in the sunroom waiting to hear what the police had to say seemed to take an eternity but, in reality, only seconds passed.

It was Sergeant Michael Baade who said: 'Your daughter Jane has been shot and is now dead.'

Helen and I looked at each other, stunned. Why Jane? The outpouring of emotion and grief seemed endless.

LADY'S DAY

With the terrible shock we had just suffered our first thoughts were for Mark at work and most of all, for the children.
* From John Magill's Diary.

SOCIETY is becoming increasingly conditioned to acts of senseless violence, but the murder of Jane Thurgood-Dove seemed to touch the broader community the way many don't.

Here was a young mother who was stalked for days by two men in a stolen car as she went about her daily routine of taking her children to school, shopping and living a normal, productive life.

The then Premier, Jeff Kennett, was personally moved by the case and intervened to double the $50,000 reward requested by police for information.

Two men in a silver-blue VL Commodore sedan had been spotted in the area in the days before the shooting and detectives believed Jane was followed on her way to drop two of her children at the nearby Essendon North Primary School.

As she pulled into the driveway of her Niddrie home the stolen Commodore pulled up, blocking in her four-wheel-drive. A man, aged in his forties, and with a pot belly, chased her around her car before shooting her three times in the head with a heavy calibre handgun.

Her children were left cowering in the car as the killer sped off in the stolen Commodore, driven by a younger, thin-faced man.

The stolen car was burnt a few streets away. The men have not been identified, nor has a motive.

Police now think the killers were waiting for the perfect moment to kill her and may have been thwarted on several previous occasions by the presence of possible witnesses.

What they don't know is why two killers, possibly paid hitmen, were so determined to kill this suburban mum.

SATURDAY, 8 NOVEMBER: The phone today never stopped ringing, with calls from well-wishers for sympathy and support, and also throughout the day friends and relatives coming and going.

Ron Iddles (the Homicide Squad Senior Sergeant in charge of the investigation) called early, around 7.30am, had a cup of tea and told us how hard the investigation was going, being short of information. I don't know what it was but this hard nosed cop did appear to be emotionally upset with what he saw in this family.

THERE was nothing special about the Magills' family barbecue on Easter Sunday, 1997, except that it was a chance to catch up with the kids and the grandchildren.

It was the sort of get-together held in backyards around Australia every weekend – often fun but mostly forgettable.

John Magill took the opportunity to practice with his new toy – a video camera. He and Helen planned to head to Europe for the overseas trip they had promised themselves as a retirement present and he thought it was better to make mistakes with the video in the backyard than during a once-in-a-lifetime holiday.

The video, filled with the typical close-ups and zoom shots of a practice tape, captures Jane's three children, Holly, Ashley and Scott hunting for hidden eggs. The Magills' three daughters are there – Sandra, the eldest, Susan, and Jane, the youngest. So too is Jane's husband, Mark, and Susan's husband, Steve.

Jane is wearing a green top and black skirt, the same clothes she wore when she was photographed about two weeks earlier at her birthday. That picture now sits on the Magill's glass coffee table and is always published in the newspapers when there is a story of her murder. It's the one where she gazes at the camera and you look back, wondering why such a woman could be stalked and murdered outside her suburban home. But on that Easter Sunday that nightmare was in the future. For John Magill, it was a good time to practice with the camera.

It was no big deal and the tape would have eventually been used again to capture a more important event – something worth remembering. As it was, John Magill forgot about the tape and it remained in a drawer untouched.

Now it is one of the family's most precious possessions.

SATURDAY, 6 DECEMBER: Came across the video of the last family Easter gathering together in 1997, I was trying out the new camera before going away in May, the tape has given us a lot of memories of Jane and we can't believe she has been taken from us.

HELEN sits forward on the couch and John also leans closer in his comfortable lounge chair, though they are both no more than a metre from the screen. Their faces crease in smiles as they watch the family as it once was.

For the moment they can block out their loss and wrap themselves in the protective warmth of nostalgia as they watch the Easter video again.

People pull faces at the camera, the kids ham it up. A watcher eavesdrops on snatches of conversation between sisters who are, or were, good friends.

Jane is sitting in a white plastic chair at the outside table. Holly is on her knee and Jane has her arms draped around her in a relaxed pose, unaware the camera is on her.

She makes all the kids paper hats. Gets up and makes an attempt to do a River Dance routine with Susan. 'We really miss her laugh,' says Helen with warmth, not bitterness.

Jane waves at the camera: 'Hi Dad,' she says. Few say anything witty when they have a video camera pointed at them.

Later the music is louder and the party moves inside. The three sisters dance in the same room where they would have danced when they were kids.

Jane stands, swaying to the music. Holly walks up and stretches her arms in the air. She wants to join in. Almost without looking Jane sweeps the two-year-old into her arms and continues to dance with her child clutched to her chest. It is the unconscious act of a natural mother.

THE shock has long worn off for the Magills. It has been replaced by bitterness, almost unbearable grief and a sense of helplessness that will not go away. If there is a more crushing burden than losing a child and not knowing the reason why, they can't imagine it.

From the outside, there is little to betray the torment that this nice retired couple in their neat Niddrie home go through every day. The garden is immaculate, with a row of flowers adding a splash of color. They are well-dressed and try to push on as best they can. They don't show obvious signs of their grief. They have been brought up to keep such things private.

But it is not private. It is front page news. Their friends and neighbours know they are the family whose daughter was murdered by a two-man hit squad for reasons that no-one knows, but many speculate about.

Inside their neat house the Magills cry every day. They won't go on any long trips in case the police have a breakthrough in the case. John has started to read crime books to try and understand more about the underworld.

Every day they look at the clock around 3.50 pm and think that was the moment their youngest girl was being chased around her own car by a man with a gun. Every day they ask why.

Few people can comprehend how their grief is doubled by

not knowing why she was chosen as a murder victim. George and Christina Halvagis understand. Their lives were destroyed when a man with a knife killed their daughter, Mersina, at the Fawkner Cemetery five days before Jane's murder.

They know there is no tomorrow and the pain just doesn't go away. Peter and Sarah MacDiarmid know. Their daughter Sarah was murdered at the Kananook railway station in July, 1990, and her body was never found.

They had to move to Queensland to leave the memories, but distance does not diminish the injustice nor bring any answers.

RON IDDLES has been a policeman for twenty-six years. He is married with children. He has worked in the National Crime Authority, the drug squad and has had two stints in the homicide squad.

He takes policing seriously and once quit the force when he felt an investigation was sold out through corruption, only to rejoin and then be fast-tracked to run a homicide team as a senior sergeant.

He is determined to find out the truth about Jane Thurgood-Dove. After more than two years on the case he was not prepared to say he knew who pulled the trigger, but he believed he was getting closer.

He has travelled down every orthodox path as an investigator and has begun to look at the unorthodox. He has used a lie detector test on two men connected with the dead woman.

One is Mark, her husband. He passed every test.

The other was a man who was (and remains) obsessed with Jane. He agreed to the polygraph test, but failed it miserably.

The polygraph is not evidence. It is not foolproof, but it may be a start. Theoretically, at least, it establishes when people are 'being deceitful.' In short, it might find liars – but can it find gunmen?

A former Western Australia police commissioner, Bob Falconer, who introduced the use of a lie detector in the search for a serial killer in Perth, believes the use of a polygraph is a sensible way to reduce the number of suspects.

Using that theory the polygraph test has so far reduced the number of known suspects in the Thurgood-Dove case to one.

But two men stalked Jane Thurgood-Dove and police believe there are others who know what happened.

Detectives have been told the handgun used in the murder was a 'loaner' provided by a gangster from Ascot Vale, unaware it was to be used to kill an innocent mother.

Several times heavy criminals have come close to passing on information. But each time they have walked away.

One has said he would be prepared to make a death-bed confession about the handgun. But, until then, nothing.

THERE is no right way to deal with tragedy, no blueprint to grief. Some people find talking a cathartic experience. Some who are close to a murder victim want to share their feelings in a prime time, multi-channel wake.

But the Magills are not like that. Their natural reaction is to grieve behind their wire screen security door, away from prying eyes. But they have learnt to play the media game.

They talk, not because they enjoy it, but in the hope that publicity will prick a conscience and provide a new lead for police. It also helps provide a momentary release from their constant feelings of helplessness. They have been interviewed by Ray Martin for *A Current Affair* and have appeared in press conferences organised by police.

They are prepared to co-operate with this story in the hope it may help provide a breakthrough. They know it is unlikely but a slim hope is better than none.

They have kept a scrap-book on what has been written and a

mental note on how some reporters have behaved. Two days after the murder a pair of reporters turned up at their door. They wanted an interview and a photograph. The female reporter then urged them to hurry – 'We've got a deadline, you know.'

That was the end of the conversation.

Another knocked on the door to ask if the family was related to an AFL footballer. 'I don't know how they live with themselves,' John says.

THURSDAY, 13 NOVEMBER: It is now a week since Jane's funeral ... it leaves you with a feeling of emptiness knowing there are no answers as yet.

Ron Iddles was telling us yesterday that the police were going to do a media release ... the press will probably try to talk to us. The pressure on all of us is very hard to handle.

The children must be suffering dreadfully inside being without their mother.

This morning's paper was on the kitchen table with a picture of Jane and a police report asking for any information about the two suspects in the photo fit pictures. Ashley (Jane's daughter) was at the the table and very gently put her hand on Jane's picture as if to say hello (that moment will never leave my mind) and with two fingers, pointed at the suspects and said 'bad men'. Holly saw the paper as well because Ashley said 'There's mummy.'

SUNDAY, 23 NOVEMBER: I wanted to help Jane's cause, I wanted to get on the phone and ring people, anybody who might listen. I wanted to go to the TV stations to ask for help to assist the police to catch the two responsible for taking Jane from us. It is only a short time since her parting but it seems like an eternity. I do miss her so.

SATURDAY, 27 DECEMBER: Nothing much today except Ron (Iddles) rang to say that the media wanted to speak to Mark or ourselves. They are desperate to try for a story, which they already have anyway. All they want to do is sell papers.

THE Magills are a loving couple who were looking forward to life without the pressure of running their own butcher's business. After twenty-six years at the Victoria Market and twenty at the Moonee Ponds Market this was supposed to be their time.

John is wiry and still has the muscle definition in his arms of a man who has been active all his life. He sometimes struggles with breathing and requires constant medication for asthma – a legacy from smoking the roll-your-owns he gave up ten years ago.

The house is always clean. She drinks tea and he prefers coffee but they agree on almost everything else. They know each other's thoughts so well they can finish each other's sentences with the shared speech rhythms peculiar to close married couples.

They have a daily routine that rarely changes. They eat breakfast together at the kitchen table but split the paper. He reads the news while she tackles the crossword. He takes his asthma medication and then has the inevitable sneezing bout.

They can still laugh about the little things. It is a distraction from the almost constant ache of their loss.

They don't spend every day in a black cloud of grief. They emerge from it to talk about normal events – Essendon's great form in the football, stories about their grandchildren, reminiscences about family holidays – but the conversations always return to Jane.

They should be spending these years travelling and enjoying their family. They are doing none of these things.

The family will never be the same. When they gather it is a reminder not of what they have but what they have lost.

SUNDAY, 28 DECEMBER: I'm just thinking what a close family we were and all the work to keep it that way is taken away by one evil deed.

THEY won't travel in case they miss a development and they continually verge on tears. John Magill is a tough man and his wife is stoic, but their resolve is weakening. 'I just want to be alive when they catch these bastards,' he says.

It is always with them. The newspaper says a man was caught with illegal guns; they wonder if it could be a breakthrough. They go to the local shops and see a man who looks vaguely like the description of one of the suspects. They wonder, then ring the police for an update. They don't want false hopes. They are tired of well-meaning platitudes. They want a breakthrough.

'Those who want to help us can't and those who can, won't,' he says.

FRIDAY, 21 NOVEMBER: I am alone at the moment, sitting at the table outside the back door, just listening to the birds, hearing the traffic on the freeway and quietly gathering my thoughts, looking at a family photo of Jane, Mark and the children, thinking what could have been. It is very hard to accept that Jane is with us no longer and I expect her to walk through the door. I want to believe I feel her presence all the time, the feeling comes and goes. I think she is there with me.

RON IDDLES never met Jane Thurgood-Dove but he knows more about her than her best friend. He comes to the case with compassion but also with a detective's eye for detail. He looks more for weaknesses than strengths of character because he knows from experience that identifying flaws in victims and suspects can solve murders.

Every person means different things to different people. Jane was a wife, a mother, a daughter, and a friend. She has been referred to as an 'ordinary' mum. There is no such thing.

Iddles had to break down all the little walls between roles to find out everything he could about the woman so that he could find out why she inflamed someone to the point of wanting her dead.

He has looked in every closet and found every skeleton. He found her every secret. Or has he?

Rarely has a murder created such unsubstantiated gossip about the victim. There have been stories that she was a star witness in an armed robbery case, was a drug courier or was having a torrid affair with a gangster and was murdered by another underworld figure.

None of the stories are true. It is as if we want to blame the victim for her own murder. That if she is somehow responsible then we are somehow safer. If Jane was 'just' a suburban mum who was stalked and killed then it could happen to anyone. And that means none of us would be safe.

SATURDAY, 22 NOVEMBER: I tried to have an early night, but while lying there all I could see in my mind was the terrible situation in which Jane was cast, not knowing what was going on.

The more I think about it and what happened to our Jane the madder and more disillusioned I am becoming about the law not looking after its citizens. I am so angry at the moment I just wish I could get out there and find these arseholes myself, but I would not know where to start.

It is now 10.10pm. I can't believe the information trail has stopped. It is constantly on my mind what that girl suffered and neither Mark nor myself could do anything to help her. I am trying to stay on top of things, but finding it hard.

Nobody needs to die the way she did and I looked forward to the time when the police catch these evil bastards for what they did to Jane. I look at Mark at the moment and all I see is despair.

FRIDAY, 6 NOVEMBER, 1998: *Another hard day ahead. Even though it is twelve months ago the heartache, the despair and the pain never leaves.*

MONDAY, 31 MAY, 1999: *Nothing, not a damn thing we are hearing. I think of all the good times and the best things the family was involved in. Then my mind will take me to the moment of Jane's death and I will be filled with revulsion for the two individuals who took Jane's life. Who gave them the right to make that decision? I will never give up thinking the police will get whoever is responsible. We gave Jane life, what gave them the right to give her death?*

6 NOVEMBER, 1999: *Two years to date and still no further ahead, no substantial news to get our hopes up, we patiently wait with utter frustration, meanwhile the pain goes on.*

RON IDDLES and his team have had to investigate many murders since Oaks Day, 1997, but they keep coming back to the Thurgood-Dove case, refusing to believe it is unsolvable.

They have had other detectives review the case to see if they have missed anything. They have travelled around Australia, interviewed more than a thousand people and chased down nine hundred tips. They believe the answer is somewhere in the material they have gathered.

Now the polygraph test has added some hope. It is not a breakthrough; it is just a lead, and there have been leads before that petered out to nothing. But it is a hope.

EVER polite, the Magills show you past the front door and out through the covered porch. Helen points to new shrub still in its black, plastic pot, a Camellia they will plant later that week.

'We had to get that one,' she says with a tired smile. 'It's a Sweet Jane.'